# OPPOSING VIEWPOINTS® SERIES

# Addiction

Withdrawn

# Other Books of Related Interest:

**Opposing Viewpoints Series**

Online Pornography

**At Issue Series**

Club Drugs

**Current Controversies Series**

Smoking

"Congress shall make no law . . . abridging the freedom of speech, or of the press."

*First Amendment to the U.S. Constitution*

The basic foundation of our democracy is the First Amendment guarantee of freedom of expression. The Opposing Viewpoints Series is dedicated to the concept of this basic freedom and the idea that it is more important to practice it than to enshrine it.

**OPPOSING VIEWPOINTS® SERIES**

# Addiction

*Christina Fisanick, Book Editor*

**GREENHAVEN PRESS**
*A part of Gale, Cengage Learning*

**GALE**
CENGAGE Learning~

Detroit • New York • San Francisco • New Haven, Conn • Waterville, Maine • London

HV
4998
.A343
2009

**GALE**
CENGAGE Learning˙

Christine Nasso, *Publisher*
Elizabeth Des Chenes, *Managing Editor*

© 2009 Greenhaven Press, a part of Gale, Cengage Learning.

Gale and Greenhaven Press are registered trademarks used herein under license.

*For more information, contact:*
Greenhaven Press
27500 Drake Rd.
Farmington Hills, MI 48331-3535
Or you can visit our Internet site at gale.cengage.com

Articles in Greenhaven Press anthologies are often edited for length to meet page require-ments. In addition, original titles of these works are changed to clearly present the main thesis and to explicitly indicate the author's opinion. Every effort is made to ensure that Greenhaven Press accurately reflects the original intent of the authors. Every effort has been made to trace the owners of copyrighted material.

Cover photograph reproduced by Ingram Publishing/Purestock/Getty Images.

**LIBRARY OF CONGRESS CATALOGING-IN-PUBLICATION DATA**

Addiction / Christina Fisanick, book editor.
   p. cm. -- (Opposing viewpoints)
   Includes bibliographical references and index.
   ISBN 978-0-7377-4352-4 (hardcover)
   ISBN 978-0-7377-4351-7 (pbk.)
   1. Substance abuse--Juvenile literature. 2. Substance abuse--Treatment--Juvenile literature. I. Fisanick, Christina.
   HV4998.A343 2009
   362.29--dc22

                   2008053997

Printed in the United States of America
2 3 4 5 6     14 13 12 11 10

ED071

# Contents

## Chapter 3: How Do Addictions Affect Relationships?

## Chapter 4: How Can Addictions Be Treated?

# Why Consider Opposing Viewpoints?

> "The only way in which a human being can make some approach to knowing the whole of a subject is by hearing what can be said about it by persons of every variety of opinion and studying all modes in which it can be looked at by every character of mind. No wise man ever acquired his wisdom in any mode but this."
>
> John Stuart Mill

In our media-intensive culture it is not difficult to find differing opinions. Thousands of newspapers and magazines and dozens of radio and television talk shows resound with differing points of view. The difficulty lies in deciding which opinion to agree with and which "experts" seem the most credible. The more inundated we become with differing opinions and claims, the more essential it is to hone critical reading and thinking skills to evaluate these ideas. Opposing Viewpoints books address this problem directly by presenting stimulating debates that can be used to enhance and teach these skills. The varied opinions contained in each book examine many different aspects of a single issue. While examining these conveniently edited opposing views, readers can develop critical thinking skills such as the ability to compare and contrast authors' credibility, facts, argumentation styles, use of persuasive techniques, and other stylistic tools. In short, the Opposing Viewpoints Series is an ideal way to attain the higher-level thinking and reading skills so essential in a culture of diverse and contradictory opinions.

In addition to providing a tool for critical thinking, Opposing Viewpoints books challenge readers to question their own strongly held opinions and assumptions. Most people form their opinions on the basis of upbringing, peer pressure, and personal, cultural, or professional bias. By reading carefully balanced opposing views, readers must directly confront new ideas as well as the opinions of those with whom they disagree. This is not to simplistically argue that everyone who reads opposing views will—or should—change his or her opinion. Instead, the series enhances readers' understanding of their own views by encouraging confrontation with opposing ideas. Careful examination of others' views can lead to the readers' understanding of the logical inconsistencies in their own opinions, perspective on why they hold an opinion, and the consideration of the possibility that their opinion requires further evaluation.

## Evaluating Other Opinions

To ensure that this type of examination occurs, Opposing Viewpoints books present all types of opinions. Prominent spokespeople on different sides of each issue as well as well-known professionals from many disciplines challenge the reader. An additional goal of the series is to provide a forum for other, less known, or even unpopular viewpoints. The opinion of an ordinary person who has had to make the decision to cut off life support from a terminally ill relative, for example, may be just as valuable and provide just as much insight as a medical ethicist's professional opinion. The editors have two additional purposes in including these less known views. One, the editors encourage readers to respect others' opinions—even when not enhanced by professional credibility. It is only by reading or listening to and objectively evaluating others' ideas that one can determine whether they are worthy of consideration. Two, the inclusion of such viewpoints encourages the important critical thinking skill of objectively evaluating an author's credentials and bias. This evaluation will illuminate an author's reasons for taking a particular stance on an issue and will aid in readers' evaluation of the author's ideas.

It is our hope that these books will give readers a deeper understanding of the issues debated and an appreciation of the complexity of even seemingly simple issues when good and honest people disagree. This awareness is particularly important in a democratic society such as ours in which people enter into public debate to determine the common good. Those with whom one disagrees should not be regarded as enemies but rather as people whose views deserve careful examination and may shed light on one's own.

Thomas Jefferson once said that "difference of opinion leads to inquiry, and inquiry to truth." Jefferson, a broadly educated man, argued that "if a nation expects to be ignorant and free . . . it expects what never was and never will be." As individuals and as a nation, it is imperative that we consider the opinions of others and examine them with skill and discernment. The Opposing Viewpoints Series is intended to help readers achieve this goal.

*David L. Bender and Bruno Leone,*
*Founders*

# Introduction

*"The most effective way to reduce alcohol abuse is simply to tell the truth and make sure that young people understand the facts."*

*Professor David J. Hanson,*
*State University of New York*

In recent years the debate over the legal drinking age has intensified as reports of binge drinking among college students raised concerns about the well-being of underage drinkers. In fact, in an effort to decrease alcohol abuse on college campuses, a group of nearly 100 college presidents have joined together to encourage lawmakers to lower the drinking age from twenty-one to eighteen. According to this group, known as the Amethyst Initiative, "twenty-one is not working." On the other hand, many parents, community leaders, and other college administrators argue that reducing the drinking age to eighteen will lead to higher rates of drunk driving and to adolescents consuming alcohol at even younger ages. Given that the connection between binge drinking and alcoholism is not well understood, this issue certainly deserves more scrutiny.

Binge drinking is generally defined as consuming excessive amounts of alcohol in one sitting. The National Institute of Alcohol Abuse and Alcoholism (NIAAA) defines binge drinking as "consuming five or more drinks (male), or four or more drinks (female), in about two hours." Although most experts accept this definition, not everyone agrees that binge drinking among college students is on the rise. For example, a 2005 study conducted by the National Survey on Drug Use and Health reports that two out of five college students binge drink regularly, which is up from one out of five just two decades ago. On the other hand, recent studies on college drinking conducted by Dr. David Hanson of the State University of New York and Dr. Ruth Engs of Indiana University have revealed that the number of episodes of binge drinking among college-aged students has declined over the past twenty years, while the number of young adults abstaining from alcohol has increased.

Despite these conflicting views of the prevalence of binge drinking, few educators and substance abuse researchers would argue that drinking is not a problem on college campuses. Understanding how best to deal with the issue is the greater source of controversy. In 1984 pressure from community activist groups such as Mothers Against Drunk Driving (MADD) lead to Congress passing a law that would allow the federal government to restrict 10 percent of highway funds from states that did not raise their drinking ages to twenty-one. Researchers such as Alexander Wagenaar of the University of Florida argue that this legislation "has substantially reduced the amount of drinking and the amount of damage due to drinking." Not everyone agrees, however. In fact, many researchers have begun to advocate for lowering the drinking age to eighteen. According to Barrett Seaman, author of *Binge: What Your College Student Won't Tell You*, "If you lower that drinking age—make drinking no longer a forbidden fruit but rather something that younger adults do with older adults who have learned how to handle alcohol responsibly—then you reduce those behaviors rather than increase them."

To further confuse the issue, the evidence about the long-term effects of binge drinking is also up for debate. While sources agree that binge drinking can lead to mental instability, engagement in risky social behaviors such as unsafe sex, and alcohol poisoning, it remains unclear whether alcohol abuse during adolescence and early adulthood leads to alcoholism. In fact, a 1995 study conducted by NIAAA reveals that binge drinking often begins as early as thirteen years of age, increases during adolescence, peaks in early adulthood (eighteen to twenty-two), and then gradually declines thereafter. However, the National Institute of Child Health and Human Development (NICHD) recently reported the results of a longitudinal study following the drinking habits of 11,000 children born in 1970. Participants who self-identified as binge drinkers at age sixteen were far more likely to become alcoholics by age thirty.

Whether lowering the drinking age to eighteen is the answer to youth problem drinking and future alcoholism will no doubt continue to be debated in the years to come. In any case, the general public seems unwilling to take the risk. A 2007 Gallup Poll reveals that 77 percent of Americans are against lowering the drinking age. The authors in *Opposing Viewpoints: Addiction* debate current views on various kinds of addiction in the following chapters: What Is Addiction? How Can Addictions Be Prevented? How Do Addictions Affect Relationships? and How Can Addictions Be Treated? In the end, understanding the causes of addiction may be even more important than determining ways to treat it.

OPPOSING
VIEWPOINTS®
SERIES

CHAPTER 1

# What Is Addiction?

# Chapter Preface

A recent article in *Marie Claire* asks readers of the well-known fashion magazine, "Are you tanorexic?" According to author Elizabeth Flahive, a growing number of people are reporting addiction to ultraviolet (UV) rays absorbed through continuous tanning. Citing recent research from Wake Forest University Baptist Medical Center, Flahive reveals that so-called tanorexics suffer from addiction similar to that experienced by drug addicts. For example, when forced to give up the sun, they experience withdrawal symptoms such as nausea, dizziness, and body tremors. Although this research will likely open doors to more studies on addiction, some skeptics wonder if in the quest to understand troubling human behavior the true nature of addiction is sometimes clouded.

Self-help author Judith Wright refers to non-drug addictions as "soft addictions." In *The Soft Addiction Solutions*, she states, "Soft Addictions are those seemingly harmless habits like overshopping, overeating, watching too much TV, procrastinating—that actually keep us from the life we want. They cost us money, rob us of time, numb us from our feelings, mute our consciousness, and drain our energy. And we all have them." She refers to a variety of everyday behaviors when done without thought or focus as being addictions, including endlessly surfing the Internet, being habitually late, continuously complaining, and drinking too much coffee. Although she concedes that these behaviors can be a healthy part of anyone's life, when they begin to interfere with a person's overall sense of fulfillment then they become self-defeating.

Although previous definitions of addiction did not allow for the inclusion of compulsive actions involving other persons (sex addiction) and behaviors (Internet addiction), new understandings of human physiology and brain chemistry have made some researchers broaden the scope of addiction, which would also include Wright's soft addictions. For years, the concept of addiction included abuse of drugs and alcohol, and only recently have addiction authorities revised the concept. According to Connie Limon of Disabled World, "An addiction of any type is readily recognized by the fact that it is not a matter of choice. Individuals who are addicts do not have the ability to decide to stop abusing."

Not everyone agrees with these broad views of addiction. Most national organizations continue to restrict their definitions of addiction to include drug and alcohol abuse only. For example, the National Institute on Drug Abuse (NIDA) defines addiction as "a chronic, often relapsing brain disease that causes compulsive drug seeking and use despite harmful consequences to the individual who is addicted and to those around them." Even though some organizations have expanded their labels of addiction to apply to compulsive behaviors such as gambling and sex, most are still unwilling to classify overuse of the Internet and excessive shopping as being in the same category as substance-related addictions.

As researchers continue to study addictions, more discoveries will surely lead to a deeper understanding of how addiction works. Each groundbreaking study reveals another part of the puzzle with the end goal being a cure. Like the authors in the following chapter, all parties involved want to liberate addicts from whatever substance or behavior is affecting their lives. The first step to that freedom is understanding.

> *"No single set of factors adequately rep-resents the multi-factorial causes of ad-diction."*

# An Operational Definition of Addiction

## Howard J. Schaffer

*In the following viewpoint Howard J. Schaffer, director of the Division on Addictions at Harvard Medical School and author of several books, discusses contemporary ways of thinking about the subject of addiction. He stresses that addiction is about the relationship between the person and the object of their addiction. Although researchers have yet to come to an agreement on the nature of addiction and its many manifestations, Schaffer calls for the development of an agreed upon operational definition of addiction, which will allow scientists, health care practitioners, and lawmakers the ability to better understand and treat pa-tients.*

As you read, consider the following questions:

1. What are some fields of study that explore definitions of addiction?

2. How is neuroadaption different than addiction?

3. What are the three Cs of addiction?

Addictive behaviors represent confusing and complex patterns of human activity. These behaviors include drug and alcohol abuse, some eating disorders, compulsive or pathological gambling, excessive sexual behaviors, and other intemperate behavior patterns. These behaviors have defied explanation throughout history. In this essay, I will attempt to clarify the nature of addiction and provide an introduction to the field of addictive behaviors.

The field of addictions rests upon a variety of disciplines. Medicine, psychology, psychiatry, chemistry, physiology, law, political science, sociology, biology, and witchcraft have all influenced our understanding of addictive behavior. Most recently, biological explanations of addiction have become popular. These approaches seek to understand alcoholism, for example, by identifying the genetic and neurochemical causes of this problem. It is interesting to recognize that as we understand more about the biology of addiction, social and cultural influences become more—not less—important. To illustrate, not everyone who is predisposed genetically to alcoholism develops the disorder. Some people who are not prone bio-genetically to alcoholism or other addictions will acquire the condition. Therefore, social and psychological forces will remain very important in determining who does and who does not develop addictive behaviors.

Now it is common to think of drugs as "addictive." Warning labels inform us that tobacco is an addictive substance. We think of heroin and cocaine as addictive. Yet, addiction is not simply a property of drugs, though drugs are highly correlated with addiction. Addiction results from the relationship between a person and the object of their addiction. Drugs certainly have the capacity to produce physical dependence and an abstinence syndrome (e.g., neuroadaptation). New evidence suggests that neuroadaptation also results from addictive behaviors that do not require ingesting psychoactive substances (e.g., gambling).

Altlhough neuroadaptation (i.e., tolerance and withdrawal) can result from a variety of repetitive behaviors, neuroadaption is not the same as addiction. If neuroadaptation and its common manifestation of physical dependence were the same as addiction, then it would be incorrect to consider pathological gambling as an addictive behavior. It would be inaccurate to talk about sex and love addicts. Many people who use narcotics as post-operative pain medications never display addictive behavior even though they have became dependent physically on these psychoactive substances. Stopping drug abuse will not end addiction, since addictive behavior patterns (e.g., gambling) can exist in the absence of drug abuse. Addiction is not simply a qualitative shift in experience, it is a quantitative change in behavior patterns: things that once had priority become less important and less frequent behaviors become dominant. Addiction represents an intemperate relationship with an activity that has adverse biological, social, or psychological consequences for the person engaging in these behaviors.

## Confusion About the Definition of Addiction

Absent a clear definition of addiction, researchers will continue finding it very difficult to determine addiction prevalence rates, etiology [causes or origins], or the necessary and sufficient causes that stimulate recovery. Absent a working definition of addiction, clinicians will encounter diagnostic and treatment matching difficulties. Satisfactory treatment outcome measures will remain elusive. Without a functional definition of addiction, social policy makers will find it difficult to establish regulatory legislation, determine treatment need, establish health care systems, and promulgate new guidelines for health care reimbursement.

Scientists and treatment providers are not the only ones with a problem when the meaning of addiction is fuzzy. The average citizen will find that, without a clear definition of addiction, the distinctions among an array of human characteristics (e.g., interest, dedication, attention to detail, craving, obsession, compulsion and addiction) will remain blurred. Finally, the contemporary conceptual chaos surrounding addiction must be resolved to clarify the similarities and differences—if these exist—between process or activity addictions (e.g., pathological gambling, excessive sexual behavior) and psychoactive substance using addictions (e.g., heroin or alcohol).

## Conflicting Terminology

In response to my preceding comments, some clinicians, researchers and policy makers may argue that they indeed have an explicit definition of addiction. Since these individuals have a model, they incorrectly assume that they also have the truth; they assume that their model is accurate. In addition, they incorrectly assume that their model will work for the rest of us if only we could see the light. However, this is the problem with worldviews in general and scientific paradigms in particular: as a conceptual schema organizes one person's thoughts, simultaneously, it blinds that person to alternative considerations. Rigid thinking sets in and science fails to progress until anomalies challenge the conventional wisdom.

Absent a consensual definition of addiction, clinicians and social policy makers often are left to debate whether patients who use drugs also "abuse" drugs. Treatment programs regularly mistake drug users and "abusers" for those who are drug dependent. Too often the result is unnecessary hospitalization, increased medical costs, and patients who learn to distrust health care providers; alternatively, absent a precise definition of addiction, some patients fail to receive the care they require. As a result of these complex conditions, practice guidelines in the addictions are equivocal and health care systems experience management and reimbursement chaos. [Although a full discussion of this matter is beyond the scope of this essay, it also is important to note that not all people with addiction are impaired in every aspect of their daily life. Despite some exceptions, substance addictions tend to be more broad-spectrum disorders while pathological gambling tends to be a more narrow-spectrum disorder.]

Even under most established constructions of addiction, not all drug dependent patients evidence addictive behavior. For example, in most civilized countries, under nearly all traditional circumstances, people who are nicotine dependent do not evidence addiction with its attendant anti-social behavior pattern. When tobacco is recast as a socially or legally illicit substance, however, these antisocial aspects of addictive behavior have emerged.

Complicating matters, neuroadaptation and physical dependence can emerge even in the absence of psychoactive drug use. For example, upon stopping, pathological gamblers who do not use alcohol or other psychoactive drugs often reveal physical symptoms that appear to be very similar to either narcotics, stimulants, or poly-substance withdrawal. Perhaps repetitive and excessive patterns of emotionally stirring experiences are more important in determining whether addiction emerges than does the object of these acts.

If addiction can exist with or without physical dependence, then the concept of addiction must be sufficiently broad to include human predicaments that are related to both substances and activities (i.e., process addictions). Although it is possible to debate whether we should include substance or process addictions within the kingdom of addiction, technically there is little choice. Just as the use of exogenous substances precipitate impostor molecules vying for receptor sites within the brain, human activities stimulate naturally occurring neurotransmitters. The activity of these naturally occurring psychoactive substances likely will be determined as important mediators of many process addictions.

We may be able to advance the field by considering the objects of addiction to be those things that reliably and robustly shift subjective experience. The most reliable, fast-acting and robust "shifters" hold the greatest potential to stimulate the development of addictive disorders. In addition, the strength and consistency of these activities to shift subjective states vary across individuals. Currently, we cannot predict with precision who will become addicted. Nevertheless, psychoactive drugs and certain other activities like gambling, exercising, and meditating will correlate highly with shifting subjective states because these activities reliably influence experience—and therefore neurochemistry. Consequently, psychoactive drug use and other activities (e.g., gambling) that can potently and reliably influence subjective state shifts will tend to be ranked high among the full range of activities that can associate with addictive behaviors.

## Objects of Addiction

To this point, I have implied tacitly that simply using drugs or engaging in certain activities do not cause addiction. Now let me be explicit: from a logical perspective, the objects of addiction are not the sole cause of addictive behavior patterns. . . . If drug using were the necessary and sufficient cause of addiction, then addiction would occur every time drug using was present. Similarly, if drug using was the only cause of addiction, addictive behaviors would be absent every time drug using was missing. However, as I described before, neuroadaptation and pathological gambling are often present when drug using is absent. Therefore, either drug using is not a necessary and sufficient cause to produce addiction or gambling disorders are not representative of addictive behaviors. Furthermore, using psychoactive drugs may not be a primary cause of addiction. Even though drug using is highly correlated with addiction—because psychoactive substances reliably shift subjective experiences—drug taking is neither a necessary nor a sufficient cause of addiction. Pathological gambling and excessive sexual behaviors that do not fall within the domain of obsessive compulsive disorders reveal that addiction can exist without drug taking. These observations serve to remind us that the objects of addiction do not fully explain the emergence of addiction. Consequently, scientists need to develop a model of addiction that can better account for a more complex relationship between a person who might develop addiction and the object of their dependence. One strategy for developing a new model is to emphasize the relationship instead of either the attributes of the person struggling with addiction or the object of their addiction.

To emphasize the relationship between the addicted person and the object of their excessive behavior serves to remind us that it is the confluence of psychological, social and biological forces that determines addiction. No single set of factors adequately represents the multi-factorial causes of addiction. Unfortunately, the parameters of this unique relationship also are difficult to define. Therefore, until experience provides more insight into the synergistic nature of these factors and helps us determine the interactive threshold(s) that may apply, we are forced to operationalize addiction so that researchers, clinicians and policy makers can share a common perspective.

## A Simple Behavioral Model

In the field of addictions, workers need precise operational definitions. To avoid confusion, researchers and clinicians have developed handy operational schemes to reduce inconsistency. One simple model for understanding addiction is to apply the three Cs:

- Behavior that is motivated by emotions ranging along the **Craving** to **Compulsion** spectrum

- Continued use in spite of adverse consequences and

- Loss of Control. . . .

As a young science, the addictions represents a growing body of knowledge and a variety of emerging biological and social science methodologies—with all of the attendant rules and regulations of science—for expanding and verifying the emerging knowledge base. If the field of addictions is to mature, as have other domains of science, we must diligently work toward conceptual clarity. To develop theoretical precision, the field of addictions must escape from the cloak of partisan ideas. Conceptual clarity does not require that clinicians, researchers, and social policy makers agree. However, it does require that as addiction specialists we define our concepts and work precisely and operationally. Under these conditions, treatments and research become replicable. The full tapestry of addiction patterns begins to emerge. The freedom to explore important issues develops. Conceptual chaos diminishes and, with all of its inherent debates, science progresses.

> "Addiction is a crutch word that makes it easier for humans to dismiss their personal responsibility for choices."

# Addiction Is a Choice, Not a Disease

## Dale Netherton

*Dale Netherton is a poet, former newspaper columnist, and regular contributor to* American Chronicle. *In the following viewpoint he argues that behaviors that most people refer to as addictions are actually poor choices. He asserts that modern society willingly excuses repeated destructive actions in the name of addiction. Netherton advocates that the label addiction be abolished in favor of citizens taking responsibility for their deeds.*

As you read, consider the following questions:

1. Name one specific example given by the author that illustrates the way in which the misuse of addiction has impacted modern society.

2. According to the author, who benefits from a society obsessed with mislabeling poor habits as addictions?

3. What two options do people have when it comes to making choices?

It seems every time someone thinks they can't reverse a choice they've made, they attach the word "addiction" to their behavior and that is supposed to exonerate them from making a choice to discontinue what they claim they can't help doing. This illegitimate use of the word "addiction" leads to a myriad of behaviors that require sympathizers claiming to offer support and counseling to these hapless souls that need reenforcement of their mistaken notions.

This phenomena has permeated the highest office in the land under the banner of "an oil addiction." It has permeated the annals of nutrition with [actress] Muriel Hemingway's notion that there exists an addiction to sugar. There may be such a thing as something that is preferable (such as a dreamy state of consciousness) to facing the hard reality of life with personal responsibility but the notion of addiction negates a fundamental aspect of human nature. That fundamental aspect is the reality of making choices.

## Repeated Behaviors

When a person chooses to do something the first time it is not an addiction. A one time trial doesn't fit the definition of addiction. It is repeated behavior that latches onto the addiction label. Now rationally, how can an initial choice be exempt from poor behavior and a second choice and a third and a fourth, etc. suddenly be categorized as something that choice cannot conquer? How many poor choices does it take for a category of addiction to be proven?

There are many people who quit smoking "cold turkey". Are they then "addicted" to abstaining? Are the only people not addicted to oil the Amish and pedestrians? Are we addicted to ascribing the word "addiction" to every choice that gets repeated over and over again as if initial choice is a choice, but subsequent choices resulting in the same result aren't? It is time to assess whether we are trying to create a culture of dependent consciousness via the notion of "I can't help myself".

## Addiction Labels Deny Self-Efficacy

To deny people's regularly demonstrated ability to reduce or cease self-debilitating behaviors, no matter how powerfully embedded in their lives, is to minimize the opportunity and the fact of change in smoking, drinking, drug use and so on, even for those reckoned to be addicted by diagnostic tools. That people retain tremendous discretion in attacking addictions is critical for our public health and treatment efforts, which should both recognize and support—indeed, treatment should build on—such self-efficacy.

*Stanton Peele, "Addiction-Choice or Disease,"*
Psychiatric Times, *February 2003.*

Consider the fact that no one yet has identified their propensity to be a couch potato as an addiction to laziness. This phenomena is explained by the retort, "but I don't like physical activity," not, "I can't help myself that I'm too lazy to exercise and I'm addicted to inactivity". If you can't help yourself by what you do, how can you avoid not helping yourself by what you do not do? The reality of choice dominates what you choose to do or not to do. And all the crutches for cognitive evasion will not change this. Any person can choose to quit smoking, quit overeating, start exercising, drink in moderation, drive carefully (by choosing to focus on the road and conditions), show up to work on time, avoid drug use and a myriad of other choices that are being categorized and excused by the notion of dependent addiction.

The foundation of this addiction to "addiction" is a choice to excuse a continuance of a poor choice by avoiding personal responsibility for consequences the continuing poor choices produce. It is a desire for dependence. "I can't overcome my drinking, smoking, drug usage but if someone or something that is not me can help me I may be able to". "But I can't do it on my own". Nonsense. You made the initial choice and you can make subsequent choices. Your emotions may not agree with you but who programmed these emotions? No body is born with a craving to smoke. Smoking must be started and continued by a choice to buy cigarettes, carry matches or a lighter, find a smoking area to "light up" and grind out a butt on the sidewalk or toss it in the ash tray. Did you ever hear a smoker claim "he couldn't help it that he littered the ground with butts"?

## Addiction Is a Crutch

Addiction is a crutch word that makes it easier for humans to dismiss their personal responsibility for choices. But to rely on such a crutch word is also a choice. There are people who take personal responsibility and those who seek to avoid it. There are people who admit making a poor choice and try to correct it and there are those who claim they are not choosing to act bad "but they can't help themselves". This the morality of altruism creates for those who want others to sanction and help them with that which they don't want to deal with. Simultaneously it gives a job to those who assume a role for helping those who cannot help themselves (or won't). Addiction creates a class of dependency for those looking for new clients based on their notion of what "being good" consists of i.e helping others. Rationally helping others should rest on the idea that the others are deserving. Altruists seek out the undeserving because in their minds they need help more. If need were a valid criteria and sacrifice truly virtuous there would be many more Albert Schweitzers [a philosopher-theologian who emphasized the power of positive thinking] instead of political advocates of Socialism. So much for the integrity of altruists.

Each person has a choice making mechanism called their mind. They can either train it by learning the rules of good decision-making or they can simply indulge their emotions and equate their feelings with their thinking apparatus. This is a choice. If you declare, "I can't help how I think" You are declaring that your life is a series of personal events that you have no control over. This is a choice you make about the kind of life you will live. If you want to make things happen make choices that lead in that direction. If you want to leave it to others to make things happen and you simply will acquiesce then expect disappointment from choosing this course of action. Life for humans rests on choices they make and there is nothing that can negate this fundamental part of their nature. The invention of false notions like addiction must be negated and rejected. And this is a choice for the reader to consider.

| "We can explain everything about addiction without having to resort to causal variables like 'bad choices' or 'addict personality.'"

# Addiction Is a Disease, Not a Choice

*Kevin T. McCauley*

*Kevin McCauley is a nationally recognized author and speaker on the subject of addiction medicine and the director of medical education at Sober Living by the Sea Treatment Centers, a family of treatment centers in Southern California. In the following viewpoint, he argues that like diabetes and other chronic illnesses, addiction is also a disease. Instead of referring to addiction as a series of bad choices, McCauley advocates for a medically rooted course of diagnosis and treatment. Using recent advances in neuroscience, he seeks to prove that there are physiological causes behind addiction that can only be remedied through medical intervention.*

As you read, consider the following questions:

1. What are the origins of the disease model for treating illnesses?

2. In what part of the brain are drugs processed?

3. What is Corticotripin Releasing Factor?

The argument *against* calling addiction a disease centers on the nature of free will. This argument, which I will refer to as the "choice argument," considers addiction to be a choice: the addict had the choice to start using drugs. Real diseases, on the other hand, are not choices: the diabetic did not have the choice to get diabetes. The choice argument posits that the addict can stop using drugs at any time if properly coerced. . . .

So when we ask the question, "Is addiction really a disease?" we are asking a question about causality: I'm seeing bad behavior, *what's the cause?* Are addicts sociopaths? Are they inherently liars, cheats, and thieves? Do they have an addictive personality disorder? Did their parents raise them improperly? Did they learn addictive behavior from a bad crowd? We have bad acts, but do we have bad actors? Or are these symptoms of a disease?

## The Disease Model

To answer the disease question, we must have a standard. What is disease? What does it take to get into the "disease club" and earn the rights and privileges that accompany that distinction? In medicine, the causal model we use to explain illness is the disease model. This model, which is only 100 years old, emerged from the germ theory described by early microbiologists such as Louis Pasteur and Robert Koch.

Simply put, the disease model says that you have an organ (bone, liver) that gets a physical, cellular defect (cells die, cancer develops, an infection sets in, a bullet whizzes through the organ), and as a result you see symptoms. You see the same symptoms in all patients with that defect in that organ, differing only by severity or stage of illness.

It is easy to see how the disease model works. Let's take a broken leg. The organ is the femur, the defect is a fracture, and the symptoms are screaming, bleeding, bone deformity, and disability. The beauty of the disease model is that it strips away the nonsense about personality and social environment. There is no "femoral personality disorder." We don't have a problem with "femur gangs." The disease model gets us to the real cause of the problem: the fracture. It tells us how to treat this patient. We do not go after the symptoms, we go after the defect—fix that, and the symptoms go away. In the case of diabetes, the organ is the pancreas, the defect is islet cell death leading to a lack of insulin, and the symptoms are the seemingly unrelated symptoms that go along with diabetes. We can't cure diabetes, but the model reveals how to treat it—we replace the insulin and the symptoms get better. It may not look like much, but the disease model is so powerful a causal model that it has doubled the human lifespan in less than a century. . . .

If we could fit addiction to the disease model—if we could show what part of the brain was involved in addiction, what the nature of the defect was, and link that defect in that organ to the symptoms of addiction, then addiction would be a disease. Everything would change. And for 100 years we've been unable to do that.

Until now. In the last few years we have finally learned enough about the brain—we have finally gotten enough pieces of the puzzle—that we know exactly what part of the brain is involved in addiction. We know the nature of the defect. And we can link that defect in the brain to the frustrating, revolting, and criminal symptoms of addiction. For the first time in the history of medicine we have some hard and fast knowledge about what happens in the human brain when it becomes addicted to drugs. There are very good brain chemistry reasons for the things addicts do. We can explain everything about addiction without having to resort to causal variables like "bad choices" or "addict personality." . . .

## Neuroscientific Knowledge of Addiction

Here is a brief summary of what we know in neuroscience about addiction:

1. Drugs work in the midbrain. This is not the part of the brain that handles morality, personality, parental input, sociality, or conscious choice. That processing takes place in the cerebral cortex. The midbrain is the amoral, limbic, reflexive, unconscious survival brain. As humans, we have a bias in favor of the cortex. We believe that the cortex should be able to overcome the libidinal impulses of the midbrain. Normally that's exactly what happens. But in addiction, a defect occurs at a level of brain processing far earlier than cortical processing. The midbrain becomes bigger than the cortex.

2. While predisposing factors are important (especially genetic burden), the primary cause of addiction is stress. We all face stress, but not all of us experience it in the same way. The stress that changes the midbrain is chronic, severe, and unmanaged. When the cortex does not resolve the stress, the midbrain begins to interpret it as a threat to survival.

3. Persistent severe stress releases hormones such as Corticotripin Releasing Factor (CRF). CRF acts on genes for novelty-seeking and dopamine neurotransmission. People under severe stress increase their risk-taking behavior in the search for relief. At the same time, the brain's ability to perceive pleasure and reward—mediated through dopamine—becomes deranged. The patient becomes anhedonic. He or she is unable to derive normal pleasure from things that used to be pleasurable. *Addiction is a stress-induced defect in the midbrain's ability to properly perceive pleasure.*

4. Drugs of abuse, whether uppers or downers, . . . legal or illegal, have a common property: they cause the rapid

release of dopamine in the midbrain. If the stressed and anhedonic patient is exposed to this drug-induced surge of dopamine, the midbrain will recognize a dramatic relief in the stress and tag the drug as a survival coping mechanism. At this point the line is crossed—from the normal drug-using or drug-abusing brain to the drug-addicted brain. The drug is no longer just a drug. As far as the midbrain is concerned, *it is life itself*. This process tagging of the drug is unconscious and reflexive. Conscious cortical processing is not involved.

5. Increases in stress (and CRF) trigger craving—a tool the midbrain uses to motivate the individual to seek the drug. For non-addicts, craving is simply an unusually [strong] desire. Even though the word is the same, it is critical to remember that craving for the addict is a constant, intrusive, involuntary obsession that will persist until the drug is ingested and the survival threat is relieved. *Craving is true suffering.* The tendency to underestimate the misery of craving is a major reason for the failure by healthcare professionals to effectively intervene in addictive behavior. Brain imaging is able to demonstrate a difference in the midbrain activity of the addict and non-addict during craving. (These scans also demonstrate a relative inactivity in the cortex.)

## Choice Argument Rebuttals

In light of this new understanding of addiction in neuroscience, the choice argument takes several hits:

- Punishment will not work to coerce addicts into making the right choice because the drug is tagged at the level of survival. Nothing is higher than survival. And so nothing used as leverage—threat of loss of job, prison, loss of child custody—can compete with an existential threat. The midbrain give the addict the

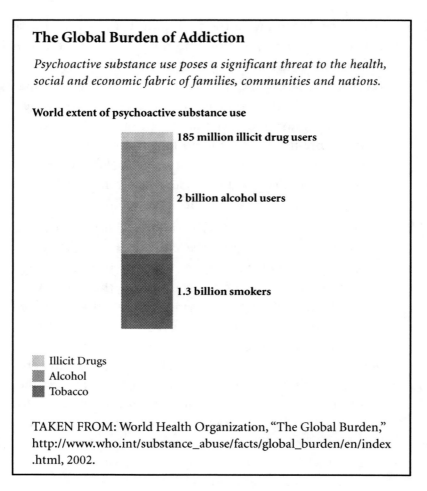

**The Global Burden of Addiction**

*Psychoactive substance use poses a significant threat to the health, social and economic fabric of families, communities and nations.*

**World extent of psychoactive substance use**

185 million illicit drug users

2 billion alcohol users

1.3 billion smokers

▢ Illicit Drugs
▣ Alcohol
▮ Tobacco

TAKEN FROM: World Health Organization, "The Global Burden," http://www.who.int/substance_abuse/facts/global_burden/en/index .html, 2002.

message that the way to take care of the children, keep the job, calm the probation officer is to first secure survival (by using the drug). When the craving really kicks in, punishment has no effect and coercion is useless.

- Addiction is a disorder of pleasure. I believe all the moral loading of addiction stems from the fact that the patient with a disorder in his or her ability to correctly perceive pleasure is much more likely to be interpreted as being immoral before he or she is seen as being blind or deaf.

- Under stress, the addict craves drugs. As far as the midbrain is concerned, the addict's moral sense is now a hindrance to securing survival. It is not that addicts don't have values; in the heat of that survival panic, the addict cannot draw upon his or her values to guide behavior. Values and behavior become progressively out of congruence, increasing stress. In order to consummate the craving, the addict's cortex will shut down. *But that's not the same as badness.* The absence of one thing (cortical function) cannot stand for the presence of another (criminal intent).

- While it is true that a gun to the head can convince the addict to choose not to use drugs, the addict is still craving. *The addict does not have the choice not to crave.* If all you do is measure addiction by the behavior of the addict—using, not using—you miss the most important part of addiction: the patient's suffering. . . .

- Just as a defect in the bone can be a fracture and a defect in the pancreas can lead to diabetes, *a defect in the brain leads to changes in behavior.* In attempting to separate behaviors (which are always choices) from symptoms (the result of a disease process), the choice argument ignores the findings of neurology. Defects in the brain can cause brain processes to falter. Free will is not all-or-nothing; it fluctuates under survival stress.

This information allows us to fit addiction to the disease model: the organ is the midbrain, the defect is a stress-induced hedonic (pleasure) dysregulation, and the symptoms are loss-of-control of drug use, craving, and persistent use of the drug despite negative consequences.

*"There is something particularly addictive, if not sinister, about role-playing games."*

# Online Game Playing Can Be Addictive

## John G. Messerly

*John G. Messerly teaches computer ethics and philosophy at Austin Community College and is the author of several publications, including* An Introduction to Ethical Theories. *In the following viewpoint, he discusses an informal study he conducted at the University of Texas at Austin. He found that many college students, especially computer science majors, suffer from addictions to video games. Messerly concludes that many players turn to gaming as a way to escape from reality. When playing becomes compulsive and harmful to the gamer and others around him or her, then it is an addiction and must be treated as such.*

As you read, consider the following questions:

1. What percentage of students who participated in the author's study stated that they knew a fellow student whose personal or academic life was negatively impacted by playing video games?

John G. Messerly, "How Computer Games Affect CS (and Other) Students' School Performance," *Communications of the Association for Computing Machinery,* vol. 47, March 2004, pp. 29–31. Copyright © 2004 ACM, Inc. Reproduced by permission of the author.

2. According to the author, when does a behavior become a harmful addiction?

3. How does the author define addiction?

Discussions with hundreds of students at the University of Texas at Austin have convinced me that computer and video games, particularly when they involve role playing, do in fact ruin the social and scholastic lives of many students. I don't claim this is the world's top social malady, but many students—particularly those in computer science at my university—are addicted to these games, and it can be inferred that students at other institutions face the same problem. The evidence for my claim is anecdotal, so it suffers from all the shortcomings of any unscientific investigation. Despite this caveat, I am convinced of the negative effect games have on college students' academic performance and social relationships.

My methodology was simple: I asked students—all computer science majors in an undergraduate program—whether they knew someone whose scholastic or social life had been harmed by computer games. About 90% answered affirmatively, describing students whose fascination chained them to their apartments or dorm rooms for days, weeks, even semesters. Many admitted to having or having had this problem themselves. The effect is exacerbated by so-called role-playing games like Age of Kings, Dark Age of Camelot, and Everquest, with addictive power so great some call it Ever-crack. Players create characters and alter egos in cyberspace, living out their personal fantasies, usually by adopting the traits they believe they lack in the real world. My informal surveys suggest there is something particularly addictive, if not sinister, about role-playing games.

Students have told me of parents withdrawing financial support from their children who play games at the expense of their studies; of intimate relationships undermined by an obsession with virtual worlds; and of roommates who no longer respond to human interaction while playing, transfixed as they are by the interface bridging virtual experience and human mind.

## Escapism

Escapism is the primary appeal. Moreover, as the graphics get better and the game play more sophisticated, playing becomes even more engrossing. It is easy to understand why anyone would want to escape our difficult and complicated world and fall into a vivid, compelling game environment. One can live there with little or no interaction with the ordinary world. With money, online bill paying, and groceries delivered to the door, one can peer almost full time into a computer screen.

Why would anyone choose to live as a character in a game instead of in the real world? Virtual reality, increasingly indistinguishable from real reality, is almost here, and many like it. Today's students are among the first generation to experience these games, and their life choices—or rather, the choice of a cyberlife—may herald the future choices of the general population.

How can I convince them not to compulsively play such games? One strategy is to point out the negative consequences games can have. Suppose they don't care. Suppose they say their lives are terrible, especially compared to their counterparts in cyberspace. Suppose further they claim role-playing games allow them to be courageous heroes they cannot be in real life or that communication with online friends teaches them something about relationships they would otherwise never know.

It is easy enough to imagine college students who don't care about their coursework and other scholarly pursuits. But a committed gamer might say that familiarity with the fast-paced computer world is actually job preparation for the 21st century. In short, if they prefer playing games to studying, finding an effective rejoinder is difficult. I could assert my preference for reading over gaming, but this would only reveal my subjective preference. Who am I to say anything about their preferences, especially when they don't seem to hurt anyone, other than possibly the players themselves? Gamers could claim that role-playing games make their lives better than the ones they live in the real world; thus, they might add, the consequences of playing are in fact positive.

## Harming Others

If gamers deny the harm games might do to them—about which they may be correct—we could argue that they harm others. For example, real-life human relationships are more difficult to maintain with people who play games, since they spend so much time chained to their computers. To this objection, gamers might say they aren't worthy of others' interest or want time alone. But even if we acknowledge the validity of such claims, what of the disappointment they cause their parents? Here, gamers might question whether college students should make decisions based on whether or not they disappoint their parents.

Parental approval/disapproval may be a consideration, but it is hardly the only or even most important one. If it were indeed the most important, how many of us would still have disappointed our parents? And how many of us would choose to live in accord with our parents' desires? Most of us would grant that personal autonomy holds sway over others' preferences, even those of our parents.

What about students who depend on their parents for financial support for their habit? In this case, parents are likely justified in pulling back from a project they deem worthless. Students who are financially independent can circumvent this obstacle. In fact, it is now possible to make a living from role-playing computer games, my students tell me, by creating and developing characters with special powers or virtues, then sell-

# Is Video Game Addiction Real?

Reports from around the world suggest that gaming addiction is real and on the rise. Nationally, 8.5 percent of youth gamers (ages 8 to 18) can be classified as pathological or clinically "addicted" to playing video games. Most youth play video games and many feel that they may be playing too much. Nearly one-quarter (23%) of youth say they have felt "addicted to video games," with about one-third of males (31%) and a little more than one in ten females (13%) feeling "addicted." Forty-four percent of youth also report that their friends are addicted to games. With nearly 8 in 10 American youth (81%) playing video games at least one time per month, including 94 percent of all boys playing, this certainly raises concerns about video game addiction.

These are just some of the results of a new survey of 1,178 U.S. children and teenagers (ages 8 to 18) conducted online by Harris Interactive between January 17 to 23, 2007. This study is the first to document a national prevalence rate of pathological video game use among youth.

*Harris Interactive, "Video Game Addiction: Is It Real?"*
*April 2, 2007. www.harrisinteractive.com.*

ing them for profit. One can expect entrepreneurs to find yet other ways to make money via role-playing and other computer games. Short of financial dependence on people who frown on compulsive game playing, there seems no conclusive argument concerning either harming one-self or others against a gamer's personal fixation. So, without good reason, we have failed to convince either the gamer or ourselves to give up a potentially addictive habit.

# The Gamer's Lament

Gamers could ask whether all role-playing games are really as bad as I claim. First, I doubt the benefits can possibly outweigh the costs in terms of personal time and energy. It is possible that games do facilitate social interaction, since many require players play together as a team and get to know each other. For the shy or the friendless, this is surely a comfort. Still, games' addictive effects—I feel justified in calling them that—suggest they may be more pleasant and engaging than real life; otherwise their appeal wouldn't be as great as it is.

In defending their habit, gamers might yet cite several more arguments:

- Most gaming experience doesn't lead to the collapse of one's social life;

- Gaming offers at least some positive lessons, especially as it relates to human-computer interaction; and

- Some gaming might actually aid a computer science education illustrating, say, the lessons of proper design for human-computer interaction.

Strong counterarguments can be made against all of them. The first concerns how much time might be spent gaming before the gamer's social relationships begin to break down. Determining with accuracy is difficult, but given my anecdotal evidence, the social and academic lives of people playing several hours a day are affected. As for positive lessons, some could involve cooperation and strategy, as well as how to design yet more games. But the fact is that games, especially those involving role-playing, target primal areas of the brain satisfying primitive needs in the (primarily male) psyche.

As for the claim that at least some amount of gaming rounds out a contemporary computer science education, I simply reject it. Students can take all the interface/game design courses they want.

## Games and the Addictive Personality

If it could be shown scientifically that gamers become addicted to role-playing games, the case against them would be stronger. Why? Because addictions involve compulsive behavior that harms the lives of the people doing it. The key to understanding why we view addictions as harmful is the conjunction of compulsivity and negativity. If only one, but not the other, is present we'd likely not refer to a particular behavior as an addiction. It may measurably hurt me to smoke a cigarette, but I'm hardly an addict if I quit immediately afterward. Likewise, I may be compulsive about many things without being addicted to them in a negative sense. I may be compulsive about eating healthy meals and exercising 30 minutes a day, but few would label me an addict. Compulsivity by itself doesn't make someone an addict—at least not in the negative sense. And the reason we aren't likely to view such people as addicts is primarily because there isn't anything negative about eating or exercising in moderation. However, if I did nothing but breath, eat, and exercise, it might be said I was compulsive in the negative sense, precisely because my behavior doesn't reflect moderation or temperance.

I have now introduced another idea—moderation—in my effort to understand this harmful addiction. Thus, I define addiction as a compulsive behavior, engaged in without moderation, that directly harms one's life.

Compulsive gamers are therefore addicts. While it would be difficult for them to deny their behavior is compulsive, they might still claim it affects their lives only in positive ways. Cigarettes, which may seem good to smokers, really are harmful to human health, independent of anyone's desire for a smoke. Similarly, role-playing games may appear challenging and fun to those playing them—because they may be so uncomfortable with or fearful of the world as it is.

We can only hope gamers begin to recognize that the real world holds much more rewards for those with the courage to face it, promising more positive experience, knowledge, joy, and love than any world of computer-generated reality.

> *"Using the term 'online gaming addiction' is a rhetorical strategy for implying a lot of conceptually misleading things."*

# Online Game Players Are Often Mislabeled as Addicts

*Nick Yee*

*In the following viewpoint Nick Yee, a research scientist at Palo Alto Research Center, argues that the media and the general public are often too quick to label video game playing an addiction. He notes that the Internet and not the user is generally blamed when someone is injured through suicide or neglect while playing online video games. While Yee admits that there can be negative consequences when game playing becomes compulsive, he points to the potentially positive aspects of gaming as well. In the end, he calls for playing in moderation and a better understanding of video game behavior.*

As you read, consider the following questions:

1. What are two similarities between playing football and playing MMOs?

Nick Yee, "The Trouble with 'Addiction'," *The Daedulus Project*, http://www.nickyee.com/ daedalus/archives/001543.php?page=8, vol. 6, November 20, 2006, pp. 1–9. Copyright © 2003–2006 by Nick Yee. Reproduced by permission.

2. According to the author, how can MMOs be socially empowering for teenagers?

3. According to the author, what are some factors that might contribute to a person developing destructive game-playing habits?

It's not easy to talk about "online gaming addiction". This is partly because "addiction" is a very loaded term. And it bears emphasizing that "addiction" is a very complicated concept. Some things, like coffee, cause physical addiction, and most people who drink coffee are technically addicted to coffee, but few people think of that addiction as a bad thing. On the other hand, marijuana is not physically addictive, but people can become psychologically addicted to it, and that can become a bad thing. Some people say they are addicted to knitting or the TV show *Lost*, but most of them are neither physically or psychologically addicted. They just use that word to imply how much fun they have with their hobby. But just because some people can become psychologically addicted to shopping or golf (or other idiosyncratic and bizarre activities) doesn't mean that these activities are addictive for everyone. Finally, falling in love is also a kind of addiction that can both enable some people while completely disabling others. In other words, the same addiction can be good for some people while being bad for others. . . .

What's clear is that there is a real problem. There's a great deal of evidence that some MMO [massively multiplayer online game] players spend so much time playing MMOs that other parts of their lives (work, academics, relationships) are severely impacted, and that they have trouble accepting they have a problem and controlling their play patterns. On the other hand, the simplistic framings and perspectives that dominate the media on this issue are somewhat misleading. And much of this is due to how loaded the term "addiction" is how it shapes discourse around online games. When shallow comparisons between online games and cocaine are made, what's left out is the other leg. And I would argue that if we really want to understand the nature of the problem (and actually help these people), we have to understand the bigger picture.

## Cherry-Picking Addictions

As big as the stereotypical jock vs. nerd divide is in high schools, there are a great deal of similarities between football and MMOs. They are both social activities that take place in a cordoned-off portion of the real world. In these virtual worlds, different rules come into play. Players take on fantasy roles that only have functional meaning in the fantasy world. They are awarded points for arbitrarily defined tasks. Cooperation and competition play large roles for players in both worlds. And it isn't uncommon for players in both worlds to develop significant relationships with others they have played with.

On the other hand, there is a tremendous difference in how people interpret tragedies that occur in these two worlds. High school and college students on football teams regularly die during practice, but their deaths are dealt with by the media with a very holistic perspective. The media questions whether the coach set an unreasonably exhausting regimen. The media questions whether the parents saw warning signs. They ask whether the school reviewed the coach's history thoroughly when the hiring was made. They wonder why the school mandates year-round practice that necessitates training in the hot summers. They ask whether the team physicians condoned the exhausting practices despite the individual's particular health idiosyncrasies. And in no time during all this does anyone suggest that football is addictive and caused the deaths. This is because that statement would be naïve and simplistic.

When people die during or after playing an MMO however, it is typically "caused by an online gaming addiction". The Wikipedia entry on "game addiction" lists several of these "notable cases". Even in cases where the person suffered from depression and other mood disorders, an "addiction" to the game itself is primarily blamed for the deaths. As another example, Kimberley Young's discussion of Internet Addiction Disorder implies that marital affairs that occur online are primarily the fault of the Internet, rather than having to do with personal choices. Why is it that explanations are complicated and holistic when it comes to football, and so simplistic when we talk about online games? Part of the reason is that football is too mainstream and too low-tech to be a tool for the media to instill paranoia with. No one is afraid of a leather ball.

We pick and choose what we label "addictions" in other ways too. For example, pedophilia is a kind of "child addiction", but no one blames children for causing the addiction. We don't argue that children are accessible, controllable, and cause excitement and thus cause "child addiction" (analogous to Kimberley Young's ACE model of Internet addiction). We don't argue that molesting a child causes dopamine increases and is physiologically reinforcing over time. We don't blame the child fashion industry for deliberately designing cute clothing that attracts pedophiles. We also don't blame shopping malls for kleptomania. I would argue that the level of social acceptance for technologies, objects, and people influences how likely we blame them in analogous scenarios, and how likely we take on holistic as opposed to narrow perspectives in trying to explain the problem.

To argue that the application of "clinical addiction" on to different behaviors is somehow an objective scientific process is to ignore the fact that all social institutions are embedded in cultural and financial frameworks that shape their beliefs and actions. Many embarrassing "mental disorders" have been included in the [Diagnostic and Statistical Manual of Mental Disorders] DSM in the past—being gay used to be a pathological behavior. Whether a novel behavior tied to a novel technology qualifies as an "addiction" is anything but a simple matter.

## Are MMOs an Ingested Substance?

When people use the term "online gaming addiction", they are encouraging others to think of online games as a kind of physical substance. This is a rhetorical move that asks the audience to ignore everything about MMOs except that they are like alcohol or cocaine. The problem is that online games aren't simply liquids or powders that are ingested. Online games are also not simple behaviors like gambling.

Online games are social worlds with their own geography, culture, dialect, and social rules. They are places where protests and vigils are held. They are places where slang and etiquette rules emerge. They are places where people meet and then get married face-to-face. And to the extent that they are social places, asking whether someone can be addicted to an MMO is like asking whether someone can be addicted to the United States. To see how analogies with cocaine and alcohol fail with social places, we can paraphrase a survey item for diagnosing Internet Addiction Disorder: "Would you become irritated and frustrated if you were unable to live in the US?"

Up till now, the label "addiction" has never been applied to a social place. It has been applied to substances and simple behaviors such as gambling. When the media and others use the term "online gaming addiction", they are asking us to ignore all the ways in which an online game is different from an ingested substance. . . .

## Getting Past Either-Or

Another complication with MMOs is that they can be therapeutic and destructive at the same time. While the media likes to describe the issue in terms of polarized pro-game and anti-game opinions, it's not clear why online games can't be both enabling and disabling at the same time. For example, some people have access to social opportunities in virtual worlds that they do not have in the real world. And no, I don't mean resurrecting the dead. Teenagers who are sufficiently mature

## Potential Benefits of Video Games

Within the extensive research on the health effects of video game usage, the discussion centers on negative effects. However, potential benefits of video game use have also have been noted. Technological aspects of video game use have been explored for decades. In 1980 the US Army commissioned an enhanced version of Battlezone (the first 3-dimensional first-person game) for training purposes. More recently, virtual reality (VR) and video games have been shown to have beneficial effects as learning aids within the health care sector. VR and video games have also been used for rehabilitation of stroke patients, to teach children about diabetes and asthma management, and as therapy in moderating certain phobias. These media are being explored for a multitude of educational uses, from assisting students in learning about various surgical procedures, such as laparoscopy, to helping researchers learn about cognitive illnesses, such as attention deficit disorders. However, the vast majority of games are developed solely for entertainment purposes, and with more widespread use, the detrimental health effects of gaming are most often the focus of research.

*American Medical Association,*
*"Emotional and Behavioral Effects of Video Games and*
*Internet Overuse," 2007. www.ama-assn.org.*

can become guild leaders and take on a leadership and management role in a group of a dozen or more adults. It bears emphasizing that this kind of social opportunity does not exist in the real world for teenagers because of how our society is structured. In the real world, teenagers aren't allowed to lead a large group of adults, set their play schedules, draft rules and guidelines, and resolve their personality conflicts. It's not hard to see why these opportunities can be seductive for all the right and wrong reasons. . . .

As with other activities in life, it starts to become clear that moderation is key. Online games can be therapeutic and enabling when engaged with in moderation, but can become disabling when someone plays too much. While seemingly obvious once laid out, this sensibility is oftentimes missing when the issue is presented by the media or anti-game proponents. A complicated "both-and" issue becomes mangled into a far more simplistic "either-or"/"good vs. evil" issue. . . .

This is also what's partly frustrating with the emphasis on "online gaming addiction". To ask whether teenagers are getting "addicted" to online games is a way of not asking why our schools are failing to engage our children. To ask why some people get "addicted" to their fantasy personas is a way of not asking how we expect people to derive life satisfaction from working at Wal-Mart. MMOs are seductive because they empower some people in ways that the real world does not. The people who we let fall through the holes of our social fabric are caught by an alternate reality where they feel a sense of satisfaction and purpose.

Creating labels such as "online gaming addiction" gives us the illusion that we've identified a new problem in our society instead of talking about the real and chronic problems in the world we live in. Instead of talking about why our education system is failing us, or why a tedious 9-5 existence is inevitable for so many, we have created a way of not talking about those problems. People who find empowerment in an unsatisfying world are labeled as "addicts". We brush aside the larger social problems by labeling their victims as deviants. And along with that, all the nuances, complexities, and multiple factors in behavioral and psychological problems are ignored in favor of a simplistic single factor model.

## No Simple Solution

The word "addiction" is loaded. It would be naïve to say otherwise. While there are more nuanced ways to use that word, such as differentiating between "being addicted to X" versus "X being addictive" for example, this is seldom the case when online games are dealt with. And people who use that term are deliberately setting themselves up for resistance. If they really wanted to help people understand how complicated the problem is, if they really wanted to reach out to the people who are having these problems and actually help them, there are other more neutral ways of saying the same thing. People will resist the label "online gaming addiction", but no one would argue that some players spend too much time in an MMO, that sometimes players develop dependencies to an MMO and the dependency can cause a severe impact on their work and relationships. And most importantly, that these people need help.

It would also help to acknowledge that oftentimes, other factors such as depression, low self-esteem, mood disorders, high stress, or traumatic events such as unemployment or marital crises can make a person more susceptible to developing a dependency on a variety of potentially destructive behaviors, including playing online games. It would help to mention that behavioral dependencies in general share many common features and predisposing factors, and that creating loaded terms for specific technologies can make it harder for people to understand and help resolve the problem when the rhetoric focuses so singularly on the technology. And finally, it would help to mention that behavioral problems seldom have simple and single causes, but rather are typically produced from and sustained by a variety of inter-related factors. It doesn't really help anyone when the entire issue often boils down to simplistic "yes/no", "good/evil" stances in media reports.

I would argue that with our current social paranoia, using the term "online gaming addiction" is a rhetorical strategy for implying a lot of conceptually misleading things. It is a strategy that asks the audience to take on a simplistic view of what online games are, a strategy that plays to the fear-mongering of the news media and parental concern with video games and the Internet. And ultimately, it is a strategy that in fact makes it harder for everyone involved to understand and help people with very real problems (particularly parents and therapists who know very little about online games). The label "online gaming addiction" encourages people to associate the underlying problem with the technology rather than (and in addition to) the person or their circumstances. It encourages people to ignore the therapeutic and enabling potentials of MMOs. It asks people to assume that MMO experiences are always limiting and unsatisfying. But the fact of the matter is that it's much more complicated than that.

| "Marijuana has substantial addictive potential."

# Marijuana Can Be Addictive

### Stanton Peele

*Stanton Peele is a psychologist and the author of several books about addiction, including* The Meaning of Addiction. *In the following viewpoint he argues that defining a behavior as an addiction is largely a function of societal attitudes and not always based in scientific reasoning. Nonetheless, Peele asserts that marijuana is an addictive substance and should be treated as such. Ignoring or overstating the addictive properties of marijuana can make it that much more difficult to prevent addiction and to treat users who have already become addicted.*

As you read, consider the following questions:

1. According to the author, addiction cannot be defined except in what terms?
2. In 1999 how many Americans had used marijuana for the first time?
3. According to recent studies, what percentage of marijuana users are likely to be addicted?

I have been defining addiction for some time, beginning with my book, *Love and Addiction*. From this initial statement, through *The Meaning of Addiction*, I have described addiction as a consequence of involvement with absorbing experiences that provide essential emotional satisfactions but that detract from people's ability to cope with their lives. Since many substances (and other experiences) fit this definition, the label "addictive" is potentially widely applicable. Whether a given substance is defined as addictive in a given society has to do with social custom and political convenience. . . .

The addictiveness of caffeine, for example in coffee, is periodically rediscovered, but ignored because people mainly don't care about addiction to this popular, legal, accepted drug (unless, occasionally, someone is trying to quit). Moreover, caffeine dependence is not considered in the American Psychiatric Association's diagnostic manual, *DSM-IV*.

An obvious redefinition—or refocusing—of the meaning of addiction occurred in the 1980s with cocaine. Cocaine was originally excluded from pharmacology's "addiction" or "physical dependence" category because it rarely produced standard withdrawal symptoms and because cocaine use tends to occur in explosive bursts, compared with the more steady consumption of heroin et al. Thus, typical categorizations of drugs in the 1960s and 1970s by World Health Organization [WHO] psychopharmacologists categorized cocaine as causing only "psychic"—but not physical—dependence (i.e., it was not addictive).

However, large-scale recreational use of cocaine by the 1980s—and proportional reports of negative consequences and difficulties in quitting the habit—seemed to demand a different view of the substance. As a direct result of the surge in cocaine use and reported problems, the definition of addiction was refocused on the intense urge to consume cocaine, particularly once use was begun, and the difficulty in terminating an individual session of cocaine use. Thus, after centuries of experience with the drug, a hundred years of medical usage with humans, and a half century of animal experimentation with cocaine, in the mid-1980s pharmacologists simply moved cocaine from the "nonaddictive" to the "addictive" drug column. . .

## Diagnosing Addiction

In short, any drug which is effective for the purposes of mood modification may be addictive, and this becomes apparent the more widely the drug is used and the more thoroughly the experiences of individual users are explored. As a general rule, addicted users come to rely—or depend—on the drug experience as an essential coping mechanism and way of navigating life. In this process the individual becomes unwilling or incapable (and these two traits/concepts can never be separated) of tolerating the absence of the experience produced by the drug. Addiction cannot be defined except in terms of an individual's incapacity to function without the drug and unwillingness to quit—that is, addiction must always be defined experientially or phenomenologically.

One study of cocaine users purported to measure the center of the brain in which addiction occurred (cocaine addicts supposedly have smaller amygdalas than non-addicts). This study is typical of its type—the subjects were cocaine "addicts" and the comparison group non-users. What about cocaine users, even regular users, who are not addicted? Designed as it is, this study (ideally) could only measure the impact of the use of the drug on the brain. Do controlled users have larger or smaller amygdalas? . . .

The actual experience of addiction, the severity of the attachment and difficulty of cessation, is an entirely individual and experiential matter. A measurement of addiction in the brain makes sense only when correlated with people acting and/or believing that they are addicted. Smaller amygdalas don't determine how intensely people use cocaine—or whether users will continue, or accelerate, or diminish, or quit cocaine. And any time a person with a smaller amygdala ceases or reduces cocaine use (the typical course for problematic cocaine users); he or she ceases to be addicted.

## Defining Marijuana as Addictive

One of the interesting redefinitions of a drug as addictive has occurred with marijuana. That is, marijuana was grouped (legally and in the public mind) with heroin and other powerful illicit drugs in the first half of the twentieth century. This image of marijuana continued through the 1950s and 1960s. In the mid-1960s and the 1970s, however, marijuana became a popular social drug among college and other youth populations. In the process, it became hard for people to take seriously the idea that marijuana was dangerous, and especially that it might be addictive. After all, people thought, they used it without damaging their lives (although, certainly, many people used it heavily, some perhaps even virtually constantly—cf. the term "pothead").

So, does this widespread cultural experience of largely innocuous marijuana use mean that the drug is not addictive? In *Love and Addiction*, I described Malcolm X's addiction to marijuana—in his autobiography he reported he was constantly and irresistibly intoxicated on marijuana—as typical of the 1940s. I then detailed the changing cultural mood which decided by the 1970s that such experiences were not possible:

> Another instructive example is marijuana. As long as this drug was novel and threatening and was associated with deviant minorities, it was defined as "addictive" and classed as a narcotic. That definition was accepted not only by the authorities, but by those who used the drug, as in the Harlem of the 1940s evoked in Malcolm X's autobiography. In recent years, however, middle-class whites have discovered that marijuana is a relatively safe experience. Although we still get sporadic, alarmist reports on one or another harmful as-

pect of marijuana, respected organs of society are now calling for the decriminalization of the drug. We are near the end of a process of cultural acceptance of marijuana. Students and young professionals, many of whom lead very staid lives, have become comfortable with it, while still feeling sure that people who take heroin become addicted. They do not realize they are engaging in the cultural stereotyping which currently is removing marijuana from the locked "dope" cabinet and placing it on an open shelf alongside alcohol, tranquilizers, nicotine, and caffeine.

But, as is true with any historical analysis, this one turns out to have been premature. Here is the director of the NIDA's read on the history of marijuana, picking up where *Love and Addiction* left off and extending through the 1990s and 2000s.

In the 1970s, the baby boom generation was coming of age, and its drug of choice was marijuana. By 1979, more than 60 percent of 12th-graders had tried marijuana at least once in their lives. From this peak, the percentage of 12th-graders who had ever used marijuana decreased for more than a decade, dropping to a low of 33 percent in 1992. However, in 1993, first-time marijuana use by 12th-graders was on the upswing, reaching 50 percent by 1997. . . . The percentage of 12th-graders who have experience with marijuana has remained roughly level since then, [and] [i]n 1999, more than 2 million Americans used marijuana for the first time. . . . The use of marijuana can produce adverse physical, mental, emotional, and behavioral changes and—contrary to popular belief—it can be addictive.

Here, this powerful government agency carefully markets against the still-popular—but diminishing—notion that marijuana is not addictive. However, rather than simply decide that a popular and largely innocuous substance (probably [the researcher] is aware of many nonproblematic, noncompulsive marijuana users, perhaps dating from when he was in college himself), he feels a need to create an additional basis for declaring that marijuana is, really, now addictive. Thus he adds to his statement, in order to signal to middle-age people that the marijuana experiences with which they are familiar are no longer applicable, "the marijuana that is available today can be 5 times more potent than the marijuana of the 1970s."

## Data on Marijuana Addiction

In a study following a cohort of 14–15-year-olds for seven years, [researcher G.C.] Patton et al. found that 7 percent were daily users at the last follow up. Women who were daily users were five times as likely to report anxiety and depression. This and other studies finding mental illnesses (such as schizophrenia) associated with marijuana use attempt to point to the causative role of marijuana in mental illness. For example, Patton and his colleagues found that being anxious or depressed in the first place does not lead to marijuana use. The argument this supports—which is one now widely made by researchers in this area—is that marijuana abuse is not itself a response to emotional problems, but rather triggers them.

Nonetheless, by the experiential model of addiction that I have outlined, some marijuana users will experience unusual or aberrant anxiety or depression, and they will find that marijuana provides short-term relief from these emotional problems. At the same time, when they use marijuana regularly in this fashion in response to emotional difficulties or stress, their reliance on marijuana to regulate their mood exacerbates these emotional problems. This is the addictive cycle as it occurs with any substance or involvement.

Since marijuana is the most widely used psychoactive substance, aside from alcohol and prescription drugs, and is by far the most widely used illicit drug, it follows that it is the illicit drug which will be relied on addictively by the most people. [Scientist M.C.] Wilson et al. compared two national studies conducted 10 years apart (1992–2002), utilizing *DMS-IV* criteria for either abuse (a less severe substance use

# Myth: Marijuana Is Not Addictive

According to the 2002 National Survey on Drug Use and Health, 4.3 million Americans were classified with dependence on or abuse of marijuana. That figure represents 1.8 percent of the total U.S. population and 60.3 percent of those classified as individuals who abuse or are dependent on illicit drugs.

The desire for marijuana exerts a powerful pull on those who use it, and this desire, coupled with withdrawal symptoms, can make it hard for long-term smokers to stop using the drug. Users trying to quit often report irritability, anxiety, and difficulty sleeping. On psychological tests they also display increased aggression, which peaks approximately one week after they last used the drug.

Many people use marijuana compulsively even though it interferes with family, school, work, and recreational activities. What makes this all the more disturbing is that marijuana use has been shown to be three times more likely to lead to dependence among adolescents than among adults. . . .

The proportion of admissions for primary marijuana abuse increased from 6 percent in 1992 to 15 percent of admissions to treatment in 2000. Almost half (47 percent) of the people admitted for marijuana were under 20 years old, and many of them started smoking pot at a very early age. Of those admitted for treatment for primary marijuana dependence, 56 percent had first used the drug by age 14, and 26 percent had begun by age 12.

*Whitehouse.gov, "Marijuana: Myths and Facts,"*
*www.whitehousedrugpolicy.gov.*

disorder) or dependence (the more severe diagnosis). They found current (prior twelve months) rates of marijuana abuse rates in the general population of .9 percent (1992) and 1.1 percent (2002) and dependence rates of .3 percent (1992) and .4 percent (2002).

## Defining Abuse and Dependence

Abuse and dependence are defined according to *DSM-IV* as follows:

*Abuse* One the following criterion: recurrent marijuana use resulting in (1) failure to fulfill major role obligations; (2) physically hazardous situations; (3) legal problems; and (4) persistent or recurrent social or interpersonal problems caused or exacerbated by use.

*Dependence* Three of the following six criteria: (1) need for increased amounts of marijuana to achieve the desired effect or markedly diminished effect with continued use of the same amount of marijuana; (2) using marijuana in larger amounts or over a longer period than intended; (3) persistent desire or unsuccessful efforts to cut down or reduce marijuana use; (4) a great deal of time spent obtaining, using, or recovering from the effects of marijuana; (5) giving up important social, occupational, or recreational activities in favor of using marijuana; and (6) continued marijuana use despite persistent or recurrent physical or psychological problems caused or exacerbated by use.

The proportion of abuse or dependence among users was quite high: Among past-year marijuana users, overall rates of past-year abuse or dependence were 30 percent in 1992 and 36 percent in 2002. Of course, the dependence diagnosis most resembles addiction. Of all users in 1992, 8 percent were dependent. Of 2002 users, 10 percent were dependent.

The authors noted that there was an increase in both abuse and dependence over the ten years, although rates of use, daily use rates, and quantities used did not increase. The greatest increases in problematic use were noted among young black men and women and Hispanic men. This finding follows a broad and deep pattern of drug addiction being most prevalent for people who lack alternative opportunities and reinforcement in their lives, such that drugs become the most present option for providing needed emotional relief.

Wilson and colleagues (writing for the *Journal of the American Medial Association*) concluded that the increased potency of marijuana caused the increase in abuse/dependence. However, it may also be that more users are aware of the addiction-producing qualities of marijuana, and that this "knowledge" itself contributed to the increase. The belief in a society that a substance can control one's body and mood makes it more likely that that substance will be addictive, and publication of findings like Wilson et al.'s can thus themselves contribute to marijuana addiction. Thus alcohol dependence symptoms were more commonly reported during a period of peak growth in awareness of alcohol's addictive qualities. . . .

## Preventing Marijuana Addiction

Like any other psychoactive substance, marijuana can be misused. In particular, since it directly and reliably modifies people's experience and emotional states, marijuana has substantial addictive potential. Researchers and theorists have produced widely conflicting conclusions about the benefits and potential side effects of cannabis use. But a spate of recent studies have identified a marijuana dependence syndrome in about 10 percent of current users. Although the political climate surrounding cannabis research may cause us to view this clinical and epidemiological research with some caution, there seems little doubt that some people develop substantial negative dependencies on the drug. They do so with perhaps approximately the same frequency as they do with other psychoactive substances, licit and illicit.

Policy decisions about dealing with marijuana are not particularly a function of its addictive potential, since more addictive drugs (e.g., cigarettes) and drugs approximately as addictive (e.g., alcohol) are legal and widely used. At the same time, it is important to at least recognize marijuana's addictiveness when contemplating drug reform measures to liberalize drug laws, for example by decriminalizing marijuana use. Such "truth in labeling" would identify marijuana's addictive potential for the benefit of its users and potential users. At the same time, it is counterproductive to overemphasize marijuana's addictiveness, since this may actually increase the rate of addiction to the drug.

Preventing marijuana addiction requires, at the societal level, creating a world worth living in and people capable of functioning in this world. Individuals who may use marijuana need to be aware of the signs of addiction and of the ways in which people avoid or reverse marijuana addiction. This involves diminishing or ceasing use through expanding and solidifying other connections to life—to people, recreational activities, work, family, et al.—which do not involve marijuana or drug use, and which in fact counteract such use.

| *"I have yet to encounter a marijuana withdrawal syndrome."*

# Marijuana Use Rarely Leads to Addiction

*Robert Volkman*

*In the following viewpoint Robert Volkman, a private practice physician in Salem, Oregon, argues that few marijuana users become addicts and that it is a far safer drug than even tobacco and alcohol. Based primarily on his own experiences as a physician, he asserts that marijuana is not as dangerous as most opposed to its legalization claim. He reminds readers that no one has ever died from marijuana use and that in some instances, such as for the treatment of chronic pain, it can actually have positive effects.*

As you read, consider the following questions:

1. What two drugs does the author believe to be gateway drugs?
2. According to a 2004 study in *The Lancet*, how many Americans die annually from cigarette use?
3. What percentage of property crimes are said to be drug related?

Robert Volkman, "Political Insanity About Marijuana and Drug Use," *Alternatives Magazine*, Fall 2004, pp. 1–7. Reproduced by permission.

Our national policy on drug use in general, and on marijuana use specifically, is simply insane. This is an inescapable conclusion drawn from my nearly 20 years as a practicing physician, and from years as a citizen of my nation observing these policies in action.

Every day I see people who either struggle with or are resigned to cigarette and/or alcohol addiction, all of this being legal and socially "normal." Others of my patients use drugs of the illegal variety, including marijuana, heroin and, especially these days, methamphetamine.

As a practicing physician dealing with substance use/abuse, I focus most of my efforts on smoking cessation. Alcoholism is also serious, but the more severe forms of alcoholism are much less common than smoking, which is dangerous even at minimal use. I have only disgust for methamphetamine, telling my patients who use it that I liken it to crank case oil. Cocaine use/abuse tends to be more an issue with a wealthier class of people than I normally see in my clientele. With heroin patients I have observed firsthand how very addictive it is, and the limited effectiveness of current treatment options available under existing methadone maintenance programs.

Regarding heroin, it is interesting to note that there are programs in Switzerland and the Netherlands (of all places!) where heroin has been partially legalized, with notable success. Under the drug policies of these nations, addicts, with access to clean needles and uncontaminated sources of the heroin, are able to lead normal lives with their families, hold down regular jobs and live without the physical complications generally associated with the drug. It is a cruel paradox that heroin in these countries is a far safer drug than either alcohol or cigarettes. Heroin is certainly much safer medically than other "hard drugs" like cocaine and methamphetamine, because these, like cigarettes, are not medically safe at any level of use.

But here is the interesting part in all this discussion. I have virtually no concern about marijuana use except for the rare individual who smokes it all of the time. (A pot-head is very much like a binge drinker, and there is always a problem with bingeing, quite apart from the substance being binged on.) I usually tell my pot-smoking patients to work to change the law that criminalizes its use. When people ask me about marijuana being a "gateway drug," I need to remind them that, on the contrary, it is cigarettes and alcohol that are the true gateway drugs, as they are far more addictive in their nature than marijuana is, and they are inevitably the first drugs used by young people, largely because they are legal and more commonly accessible than any other. Additionally, the addictive tendencies are qualitatively different. For instance, I have yet to encounter a marijuana withdrawal syndrome and I seriously doubt that it even exists in any important way; certainly not like what I have had to deal with medically in the cases of the hard drugs—methamphetamine, heroin, etc. Tobacco, interestingly, has withdrawal features quite similar to these hard drugs.

## Leveling the Playing Field

Let's begin with the rational, non-controversial baseline assumption that a drug is a drug, whether legal or not. Tobacco, alcohol, marijuana, heroin, and methamphetamine—all are drugs with psychological and physiological effects in the body. From this baseline, we can compare effects and come to conclusions. If you ask, "why is the criminalization of marijuana so crazy?" one way to answer that question is to note that there are *No Reported Deaths* from marijuana use, ever. Compare this statistic to the other drugs on the list—tobacco, alcohol, heroin, meth and the rest.

Death from drug use, whether cumulative over time or catastrophic overdose, is ugly. I have personally seen patients of mine dying from cigarettes since the time I was a medical student. Some 440,000 die every year from cigarette use in this country alone, with an estimated 10,000,000 expected to die annually by the year 2030 (according to *The Lancet* in its [July 13, 2004 issue]). Add to this the health care costs of smokers, which run into the billions of dollars, and the health consequences from tobacco's non-lethal effects that hurt uncounted others, including millions of non-smokers as a result of secondhand smoke. Yet, with all of this death and suffering, cigarettes are not only legal but the farming of tobacco has been subsidized by our government's farm policy for decades.

All deaths combined from heroin, cocaine and methamphetamine are a small fraction of those caused by cigarettes, but each one is tragic and avoidable.

With alcohol it's the same old story, though the numbers aren't so high as with tobacco. Tens of thousands die every year from the cumulative effects of alcohol consumption, with thousands more dead from vehicle and work accidents related to addictive consumption of alcohol. In addition, alcohol abuse is incredibly destructive to marriages and families. I have seen alcohol kill in my immediate family, and destroy the lives of friends close to me. In the VA [Veteran's Administration] hospitals I trained in, the wards were crowded with those suffering from the medical complications of alcohol.

It is a troubling fact that, when we consider these substances and their effects on society in an evenhanded way, we see that the most dangerous among them are also the most legal.

## Crime and Punishment?

Given the known dangers to real people and the costs to society, does it follow that we should criminalize the use of tobacco and alcohol, as we do the other drugs? Hell no!! The "moral crusade" of alcohol prohibition during the 1920s & 30s proved the folly of that course of action and was rightfully repealed—but not before crime syndicates like the Mafia [organized crime] had reaped enormous profits gained when alcohol was pushed underground. Prohibition does not work, plain and simple. It didn't work for alcohol in the 1920s & 30s, and it doesn't work for drugs today. It is the wrong way to deal with problems of personal choice and substance use/abuse.

Nobody disputes that these substances, legal and illegal, can be quite addictive and dangerous. When considering the social costs (pain & suffering, ruined lives, neighborhood crime, billions of dollars spent making & distributing product or trying to dissuade use, police work, judicial & prison institutions, etc.) the distinction between legal and illegal may seem irrelevant, because all of these substances have a similar set of consequences. But the distinction is not irrelevant. Strange as it may seem the illegality itself becomes one of the hardest things to deal with when it comes to "hard" drugs.

As stated earlier, I work very hard to help people stop smoking and abstain from excessive alcohol use, and I also work with people to stop using illegal drugs—meth, heroin and cocaine. I can say from experience that all of these efforts to promote health are impeded when the patient's drug of choice is classified as illegal. It would be a nightmare to confront and deal with alcohol and smoking addiction if these two substances were illegal—look how hard it is to deal with them as they are! With the illegal drugs, this nightmare is part of my day job as a physician dealing with public health issues.

And then there is marijuana. Marijuana is illegal, with billions being spent as part of a "War On Drugs" against its use. For 70 years, the propaganda about its effects has been unsupported by the science and, indeed, has been the worst kind of hubris. I have yet to see a family destroyed by use of marijuana, though I have seen great harm done to many people when legal actions have been taken against those who use it. There is virtually no medical basis for even scolding people about its use, except when they are bingeing on it, as de-

| Annual Causes of Death in the United States | |
| --- | --- |
| Tobacco | 435,000 |
| Poor diet and physical inactivity | 365,000 |
| Alcohol | 85,000 |
| Microbial agents | 75,000 |
| Toxic agents | 55,000 |
| Motor vehicle crashes | 43,000 |
| Adverse reactions to prescription drugs | 32,000 |
| Suicide | 30,622 |
| Incidents involving firearms | 29,000 |
| Homicide | 20,308 |
| Sexual behaviors | 20,000 |
| All illicit drug use, direct and indirect | 17,000 |
| Non-steroidal anti-inflammatory drugs such as aspirin | 7,600 |
| Marijuana | 0 |

TAKEN FROM: Drug War Facts, "Annual Causes of Death in the United States," www.drugwarfacts.org, May 16, 2007.

scribed earlier. I even occasionally recommend the use of marijuana, for its palliative effects on chronic disabling pain, muscle spasms of Multiple Sclerosis, nausea prevention, and such.

Marijuana, when used correctly, is highly effective for such palliative applications, but there is every indication that it has an even more profound future in medicine. It is recently reported that endogenous cannabis-like compounds, "endocannabinoids," have been found in the human central nervous system. These are similar in nature to the naturally occurring opiate-like compounds known as "endorphins" that have receptor sites in the human brain. The development of a whole range of medicines came out of that earlier discovery, including drugs used routinely for pain mitigation by doctors throughout the world. Now we know that marijuana mimics an endogenous neurotransmitter in our brains, which is a fancy way of saying that we can now pursue research that will inevitably open up a whole new field in medical knowledge and therapeutics. It certainly lends credence to the use of marijuana medicinally. In short, marijuana as medicine is real and not some fictitious rationalization for irresponsible drug use, as the federal government currently asserts.

## Public Policy

Criminalization and prohibition have obviously not worked. As with the earlier prohibition of alcohol, our criminalizing of any of these drugs has been ineffective at best and, at worst, a mistake that has exacted a terrible cost to society for nearly a century, causing untold, unnecessary human suffering. These are failed policies. As legal scholars would affirm, the propagation and prolongation of failed, unenforceable laws has the detrimental effect of destroying respect for the law in general. In a nation where we operate under the Rule of Law, this degrading effect is very significant, undermining the very foundations of this Republic.

The economic consequences of criminalizing these drugs is mind-boggling. Just try to wrap your mind around an insane distortion such as the street value of an ounce of marijuana exceeding the street value of a comparable weight in gold—and this for a plant that can be grown anywhere for next to nothing by just about anybody. Now that is a market incentive that any capitalist can understand! Many will risk the legal consequences for the financial rewards, and there are millions more who will figure out how to afford what they want to buy, even at prices that exceed gold itself. Property crime as a direct result of criminalization racks up extraordinary costs to business and private citizens (it is estimated that up to 80 percent of property crime is drug related, all brought on by our policy of criminalizing drug use). Add to this the diversion of law enforcement resources away from more important issues and the costs associated with clogging our court system with victimless crimes, and the insanity grows. Mirroring the good old days of Prohibition with Al Capone and his merry band of gangsters, whole new criminal organizations have formed and are being financed by the vast Byzantine underground economy of the drug world. But now, in this age of globalization, the problems caused by criminalization and prohibition know no boundaries, including national ones. These criminal organizations and the street gangs associated with them are a scourge to any society in which they work their dark deeds. They could be put out of business in a heartbeat if we would repeal the crazy laws that keep them in business.

Let's face it; we are an addictive culture, as witnessed by our addictions to TV, computer gaming, sex, wealth acquisition, gambling, food and even sugar (try stopping sometime!).

The criminalization of drugs, especially that of marijuana, is bad medicine, bad law, bad business, and is moral hypocrisy at its worse. This has to stop. How long will we fail to recognize and correct this mistake that is hurting so many people at such great expense? As a nation, we can live and act with much more intelligence than this. It is time to act to change these very destructive laws, changes already being pioneered in Europe. It is time for those in the medical profession and in positions of authority to speak up on this matter.

# Periodical Bibliography

*The following articles have been selected to supplement the diverse views presented in this chapter.*

| | |
|---|---|
| Joan Acocella | "A Few Too Many," *New Yorker*, May 26, 2008. |
| Mark Adams | "The Coffee Junkies Guide to Caffeine Addiction," *New York*, June 9, 2008. |
| William Baldwin | "Addicted to Debt," *Forbes*, October 6, 2008. |
| Simon Dumenco | "Are Always-Connected Consumers Really Virtual Crackheads?" *Advertising Age*, March 31, 2008. |
| Rachel Dvoskin | "Sweeter than Cocaine," *Scientific American Mind*, vol. 19, no. 2, 2008. |
| Dana Gottesman | "Food Addiction Is Real," *Woman's Day*, March 4, 2008. |
| Trisha Gura | "Addicted to Starvation," *Scientific American Mind*, vol. 19, no. 3, 2008. |
| Lashieka Purvis Hunter | "My Secret Online Addiction," *Essence*, February 2008. |
| Stuart Koman | "An Opportunity to Improve Lives and the Bottom Line," *Behavioral Healthcare*, June 2008. |
| *New Scientist* | "Internet Addiction Is a Psychiatric Disorder," March 29, 2008. |
| Jennifer Seter Wagner | "When Play Turns to Trouble," *US News and World Report*, May 19, 2008. |

# How Can Addictions Be Prevented?

# Chapter Preface

The study of human genetics has lead to a better under- standing of how the human body works. Most signifi- cantly, geneticists mapping the human genome have found clues for how some diseases are contracted and even treated. For example, a 2007 British study found several new genes linked to breast cancer. It is thought that if women know that they are genetically susceptible to developing breast cancer, then they can take steps to improve their lifestyles and their frequency of mammograms in an effort to prevent or delay getting the disease. Now that researchers have found a genetic link to psychological conditions such as schizophrenia, addic- tion specialists have begun to wonder if alcoholism and de- pendence on other drugs are inherited as well.

Despite what is known about human genetics, the direct application of such knowledge is considered limited by many experts. In the case of alcoholism, studies done in the 1970s determined that the disease is likely to be inherited in some families. Later, these results were confirmed by a number of studies, including one conducted in 2000 by the University of California, San Francisco. They concluded that 20–25 percent of sons and brothers of alcoholics become alcoholics, and that 5 percent of daughters and sisters of alcoholics become alco- holics. Linking this data to actual genetic markers has been more difficult, but researchers are hopeful. For example, Ken- neth Blum and others discovered that the dopamine D2 re- ceptor is more prevalent in alcoholics.

However, social scientists have been skeptical of those findings, wondering if environment, not biology, is really the key factor. A study conducted by Elizabeth Skiffington and Philip Brown found that children whose parents abuse drugs will be more likely to abuse drugs. Some scientists have noted that the reason these children become addicts is the result of the home life created by alcoholic parents and not necessarily genetic traits. According to Jeanne Reid, Peggy Macchetto, and Susan Foster, addicted parents often cannot maintain a stable and safe family life, which encourages their children to use drugs to cope with this lack of structure and discipline. In addition, Jiang Yu of the New York State Office of Alcoholism and Substance Abuse Services found that "the effect of perceived parental attitudes is specific to underage alcohol use." In other words, parental attitudes about drinking and drug use determined alcoholic and drug abuse among young people. If parents were lax about enforcing rules about alcohol and drug use, then adolescents were more likely to use and abuse the substances.

The National Institute on Alcohol Abuse and Alcoholism states that the risks of someone becoming an alcoholic are 60 percent attributed to genetics and 40 percent attributed to environment. If that is the case, then finding a way to prevent alcoholism requires a better understanding of both. The authors in the following chapter debate how addiction can be prevented.

| "A no-use policy is, in the majority of
| cases, doomed to failure."

# Teaching Children How to Drink Responsibly Will Prevent Addiction

*Nan Einarson*

*Nan Einarson is a certified life coach and the author of several publications, including* Do It Yourself Relationship Repair Guide. *In the following viewpoint she argues that introducing children to safe alcohol consumption at home is the best way to prevent irresponsible drinking later in life. She asserts that maintaining a total abstinence policy will only lead young people to failure and far riskier behavior when those constraints are finally lifted. Einarson insists that helping minors develop and use a system of values will prevent future alcohol abuse and misuse.*

As you read, consider the following questions:

1. According to the author, when is it too late for parents to talk to their children about drinking alcohol?
2. What is a "trust account"?

3. According to the author, what kinds of students were most likely to have trouble adjusting to the freedoms of college life?

I find this question [Should parents teach children how to drink alcohol responsibly or maintain a no-use policy at home?] to be more about how we teach our children to make responsible, independent choices, than it is about drinking alcohol, specifically. How they choose to drink alcohol responsibly, or smoke cigarettes or weed, or drive defensively, or respect curfews, or address any other challenges they may experience, are all derived from the same values system. I believe that if this question is addressed only when the children are old enough to drink alcohol, it is already too late to expect responsible decisions from them.

By teaching our children, at an early age, to make wise choices based on consequences, when the time comes for them to make decisions about alcohol, smoking, driving, curfews, etc. they will have a lot of experiences from which to draw, in order to make responsible choices. Have your children learned to make their own lunches, do their own laundry, make their own beds, take out the garbage, etc.? Are your children expected to do chores in order to earn their allowances?

When children have been exposed, from an early age, to making responsible choices and have received praise for responsible choices, they come to understand the difference between good and bad decisions, and drinking alcohol responsibly becomes a moot point.

## Establishing Trust

In our house, our children were started off with a full "trust account". That is, they knew that we trusted them to make wise, informed, responsible choices. They received positive reinforcement for their good choices and their trust accounts remained full unless/until they made a decision that resulted in a "withdrawal" from their trust account. The level of withdrawal directly related to the choice/decision. No choice was ever so wrong that the trust account could not be refilled.

Imagine if our school systems started each student off with an "A", and children worked to keep their "A" or had opportunities to recover their "A" if they made a mistake? Imagine what that perspective would do to our children's self esteem!

In our house, our message to our children (who are now grown, with children of their own) was that everyone makes occasional mistakes/wrong choices (including us, their parents). None of us is perfect, and it is through our mistakes that we learn and grow, as long as we find the lessons and try not to repeat our mistakes. They knew that our love and support for them was unconditional. Having said that, they also knew that their choices and actions had consequences, and that negative decisions/actions would have negative consequences. We would ask them what their "punishment" ought to be, and they were often harder on themselves than we would have been!

## Helping Other Kids Stay Safe

Our home was filled with our kids' friends. We treated their friends with the same degree of respect and trust and the same messages that we gave to our own children. As they got older, and alcohol became an issue, our message was always—"we hope that you and your friends will make good choices and not drink when you're underage. When you are of age, we hope that you will drink responsibly and never drive if you have been drinking". That's not to say that we ever encouraged or allowed under-age drinking, however, if it happened, their safety was our first priority.

When at our house, if anyone had been drinking, they handed in their keys and crashed at our house. Many of them

# Minimum Age Limits Worldwide

| Country | Drinking Age: On premise | Purchasing Age: Off premise |
|---|---|---|
| Argentina | 18 | 18 |
| Australia | 18 | 18 |
| Belgium | 16 beer and wine. 18 for spirits. | None for beer and wine. 18 for spirits. |
| Brazil | 18 | 18 |
| Cambodia | None | None |
| Canada | 18/19 | 18/19 |
| China, People's Republic of | 18 | 18 |
| China, Republic of (Taiwan) | 18 | 18 |
| Colombia | 18 | 18 |
| Costa Rica | 18 | 18 |
| Czech Republic | 18 | 18 |
| Denmark | 18 | 16 |
| Egypt | 18 for beer. 21 for wine and spirits. | 18 for beer. 21 for wine and spirits. |
| Fiji | 21 | 21 |
| Finland | 18 | 18 |
| France | 16 for beer and wine. 18 for spirits. | 16 for beer and wine. 18 for spirits. |
| Germany | 16 for beer and wine. 18 spirits. | 16 for beer and wine 18 spirits. |
| Ghana | None | None |
| Greece | 17 | None |
| Hungary | 18 | 18 |
| Iceland | 20 | 20 |
| India | 18 to 25, depending on state. | 18 to 25, depending on state. |
| Indonesia | 21 | 21 |
| Ireland | 18 | 18 |
| Israel | 18 | 18 |
| Italy | 16 | 16 |
| Jamaica | None | 16 |
| Japan | 20 | 20 |

**continued**

## Minimum Age Limits Worldwide [CONTINUED]

| Country | Drinking Age: On premise | Purchasing Age: Off premise |
| --- | --- | --- |
| Mexico | 18 | 18 |
| Netherlands | 16, but 18 for spirits that have an ABV (alcohol by volume) of over 15%. | 16, but 18 for spirits that have an ABV of over 15%. |
| New Zealand | 18 | 18 |
| Norway | 18, but 20 for spirits defined as 22% ABV. | 18, but 20 for spirits defined as 22% ABV. |
| Pakistan | Illegal (21 for non-Muslim population) | Illegal (21 for non-Muslim population) |
| Switzerland | 16/18, depending on the region, for beer and wine. 18 in all regions for spirits. | 16/18, depending on the region, for beer and wine. 18 in all regions for spirits. |
| Thailand | 18 | 18 |
| United Kingdom | 18 | 18 |
| United States | 21 | 21 |

TAKEN FROM: International Center for Alcohol Policies, "Minimum Age Limits Worldwide," www.icap.org, 2004.

crashed anyway, even if they hadn't been drinking, because they knew we served wicked brunches on the weekend. With brunch, they always received praise for their choice to stay in a safe place until they were sober.

When partying elsewhere, our message to our kids and their friends was always the same—"if you've been drinking and need a ride home, call us, no matter what the hour or the situation. We will come and get you and bring you home with us. No questions, no judgments—we just want you to be safe". We would get calls from our kids' friends, even when our kids weren't with them. They knew they had a safe place to go. They also knew that the next day, they would be having a discussion with us about responsible choices, and that they would be making withdrawals from the trust account with us. They also knew that by taking lessons from the experience and making better choices in the future, they could build up their trust account once more.

We always urged our kids' friends to be open and honest with their parents, because we had no desire to enable behaviour their parents would not endorse. We always encouraged them to contact their parents and update them on where they were and what they were doing, and it was amazing to us how many parents were not at home or were disinterested in where their kids were or what they were doing.

## Encouraging Responsible Decision Making

Even though I was a stay-at-home mom until both our kids were in high school, our kids would make their own breakfasts, or pack their own lunches, or come home to an empty house (they didn't know it, but I would park around the corner, to ensure that they did what they had been taught to do if they arrived home before me). That consistent trust, and our belief in their ability to make good choices gave them a solid foundation for meeting and handling difficult issues like peer pressure, drinking alcohol responsibly, and other responsible decision-making challenges.

I'll never forget, when my daughter went to University, her telling us that the students who had never experienced independence and responsibility at home were very obvious. They were the ones that went wild with new-found freedom and no restrictions or accountability. They partied into oblivion and with no self-discipline whatsoever. They were the ones who flunked out early in the school year, because they had had no prior experience with freedom and responsible decision-making.

Does that mean I believe our kids never got drunk or got high or drove irresponsibly or broke our rules? I think probably they did at some time or another—who among us has never experimented with enticing forbidden fruits? We were all young once, and we remember that we learned from experience, probably more than we did from rules, lectures, expectations and punishments.

What I know to be true is that forbidden fruits are always the most intriguing. And, the more intrigue and mystery that surrounds a forbidden activity, the more curiosity it evokes. And, curiosity almost always leads to action—action that might be forbidden, yet is so enticing it cannot be ignored. For those who have not learned how to make values-driven choices, their actions can have serious concequences.

Children will not and cannot be angels. They seek their independence, yet are very susceptible to peer pressure and their greatest desire is to fit in with their friends and do what their friends do. For that reason, I think a no-use policy is, in the majority of cases, doomed to failure.

> "A zero-tolerance policy is vital ... to
> help your children avoid the hazards of
> underage drinking."

# A Zero-Tolerance Policy
# for Teens Will Prevent Alcohol
# Abuse and Addiction

### Teen Drug Rehab Treatment Centers

*Teen Drug Rehab Treatment Centers offers an array of programs for young people struggling with drug and alcohol addiction. In the following viewpoint the authors argue that parents should not allow their children to drink alcohol at family social functions because it encourages the possibility of irresponsible alcohol use. The authors encourage parents to better understand teen drinking culture by listening to what their children and their children's friends say about alcohol use. They assert that maintaining a zero-tolerance policy regarding the consumption of alcohol is the only way to prevent future abuse and misuse.*

As you read, consider the following questions:

1. What are alcopops?

Teen Drug Rehab Treatment Centers, "Parental Denial about the Dangers of Beer and Alcopops Can Endanger Teens," *Drug Rehab Treatment: Addiction Treatment Resources for Parents of Teens and Young Adults*, pp. 1–5. Reproduced by permission.

2. According to the authors, by around what age have people learned to be responsible social drinkers?

3. According to the authors, what is the best way to prevent teens from drinking irresponsibly?

Teen [alcohol] drinking leads to so many troubles and tragedies. It is distressing that parents often fail to observe or understand initial symptoms in their children's lives and behavior. Most parents are well aware of the increasingly grim army of statistics indicating that large numbers of teens are beginning to drink heavily as soon as they start middle school, and the devastating physical, mental, and social repercussions. Yet, fewer understand the social circumstances and common misunderstandings that allow young people to begin potentially lifelong problems with alcohol with just a few beers or alcopops [flavored alcoholic beverages like wine coolers]. Getting an intimate understanding of the circumstances and pressures young people are exposed to can help families have open and effective conversations and rules about drinking.

## Deciding on a Zero-Tolerance Policy

The common belief that beer or alcopops pose less of a danger to teens is dead wrong. These beverages have been shown over and over to be a rapid gateway for some teens, not only to the strongest alcoholic beverages, but also to drugs, criminal acts, and treacherous social behaviors—like teen sexual assault and rape. Teen alcohol tolerance is generally so much lower than that of adults that even these gateway drinks regularly get them perilously drunk in short order. When lower tolerance is considered in tandem with teens' potential immaturity and lack of awareness of the myriad dangers impaired thinking brings, it is clear that alcohol cannot be tolerated in the lives of children.

It is easy to see why many parents allow their kids a beer at home or at a family event like a wedding or BBQ, especially if drinking is part of the family culture. Common misconceptions are that a drink with the family is fine because it lets teens get their first experiences with alcohol in a safe and supervised environment, helping them build their tolerance and taking away the alluring mystique of the forbidden. Also, it could often feel like it is the charitable and inclusive thing to do, if adults are having fun relaxing with a few beers together. However, this mentality can lead to confusion and a false sense of security and confidence for parents and teens. If your children are drinking with the family regularly enough and to the degree necessary to develop any kind of tolerance, they are not only developing a habit that they will almost always seek to continue on their own, but also gaining a perfect loophole to think and say, "It was cool with you when I had a beer with your friends, so why are my friends different?"

Forbidding teens from ever drinking alcohol even in the presence of family or on social or religious occasions is incredibly hard for even the best-intentioned parents. The truth is that making it completely unacceptable does increase teens' curiosity dramatically, making it more likely that they will go to their friends and the unscrupulous people who buy alcohol for teen parties, putting them at even greater risk. However, there are effective ways to empower non-drinking teens to understand why and how to say no. A zero-tolerance policy is vital in order for you to hold on to your ability to help your children avoid the hazards of underage drinking.

If you are ready to concede that your teens will do a significant amount of underage drinking, then taking the middle road may be for you. Yet, if you let them drink it can subconsciously turn their perception of the danger involved from roadblock to a speed bump. Even if you are clear with them that they may only drink when you offer it to them, it makes it a legitimate behavior for them in their minds. This makes it almost as easy for them to say yes when someone else they trust and admire offers them a drink.

## Alcopops Are Harmful

Alcopops are a commonly overlooked threat to keeping teens, especially girls, sober. Drinks like Smirnoff Ice, Mikes Hard Lemonade, and Sparks are made and marketed to get young teens started drinking. Because they taste similar to soda, deliberately masking the taste of alcohol from the taste buds, they go down easily. Young teens unaccustomed to the taste of beer and alcohol can get started without even thinking about it. Just as threatening, because they do not taste the alcohol many inexperienced drinkers often do not realize the alcohol's effects until they are too tipsy to make clear decisions. Alcopops that include large amounts of caffeine, like Sparks, are especially risky—not only because the caffeine gets the alcohol into their blood stream even quicker, but also because the combination of the two makes for a hyperactive drunk who is even more likely to keep up the energy for reckless acts.

Parents should not need the plethora of pointed studies to see what the alcohol companies are up to. The advertisements feature attractive young women getting what they want socially, and are aired during TV programs counting on a teen audience. These companies know that if they can get girls to drink at an earlier age the guys will not hesitate to get alcohol for them. Even more appalling, if young teens can get alcopops, they can get cheap strong liquor. It doesn't take long to move from the gateway drinks to the hard stuff. Just mix it with soda and it is like an Alcopop, but three times as strong.

## Teen Drinking Culture

What many parents misunderstand is that most teens drink for very different reasons and in very different ways than their parents. Many adults who drink do so to complement a good meal or just to relax after a long day or with friends. Most parents have learned by the time they have teenagers that setting out to get drunk is a mistake that usually leads to more mistakes. If not, this is something one hopes that they will ad-

"Well—aren't you going to ask me if I'm over eighteen?" Cartoon by Dave Parker. www.CartoonStock.com.

dress themselves. Essentially, by middle age most people have figured out how to be social drinkers long enough ago that they may lack a tight grasp on what it is like for teens beginning to drink under today's different and more dangerous circumstances.

Even just drinking beer or alcopops, the vast majority of teens are not seeking to relax anything but their inhibitions—and those of the people around them. Let's be clear, they are most often seeking to get wildly drunk. Young people are at such an increased risk of alcohol poisoning, not only because of their lower tolerance, but also because drinking until they deliriously throw up and pass out is so often seen as a badge of honor in their peer groups. At the very least it is something to be laughed off and notoriously joked about for weeks, and repeated regularly.

Most parents who drink would be likely to see this kind of repeated behavior in their peer group as a grave sign of an unhealthy life and mindset. So it is easy to see why they may not fully realize that so many teens hold a directly opposite view, believing that getting drunk is a normal way to have a healthy social life.

If you have not seen plenty of examples that teens broadly look at drinking this way, you can ask people in your community who deal with the aftermath: police, school counselors, and most importantly, the teens in your life. Perhaps the easiest way to get a grip on this view is to take a few minutes to peruse legions of photos and stories young teens post on the Internet of themselves falling down drunk, especially on Myspace. Even if your kids and their friends have not done this, it is likely that a good number of young people at their school and in the area have.

Why do young people think and act like this so much more commonly now than was the case when their parents were kids? It is largely a subjective question. You can blame any combination of cultural changes. MTV, explicit music lyrics, and the messages young people get from the media doubtless play a major role. Parents are working more and are less able to spend time with their kids. The dramatically increased marketing of alcohol to teens, and the declining role of religious beliefs and community in young people's lives have a pronounced impact on alcohol consumption. The parents in the *Brady Bunch* did not drink much but Homer Simpson sure does.

## Listening to Teens Who Drink

Since it is unlikely that parents can protect their kids from most of the circumstances of our changing times, it is critical that adults learn to listen to the stories that these conditions often spur young people to tell themselves and their friends over and over again, until they live by them. A general sketch of the part of these stories directly about drinking commonly sounds something like this:

> "When we get drunk, crazy fun things happen, people do hilarious stuff and get to be themselves. People stop being awkward and just hook up. I'm having a new different kind of fun than when I was a little kid, because I'm totally different now and I really want to see what it's like to party like a rock star. So I sneak out and get drunk when I get a chance—that's what the people my friends and I want to hang out with do. Sure it's a little insane. Thank goodness we don't remember half of it."

It would be surprising to hear this belief system articulated by sober teens talking to their parents, but if you log into a couple teen chat rooms you can observe them trumpeting it to their friends. The clearest fundamental way to prevent teen drinking from getting started is to be sure that they have a healthier self-narrative about alcohol to begin with, even about beer or alcopops. Once teens start to believe, personalize, and repeat, this kind of story, many parents feel they have to try to upend their teen's world view and be a police officer 24/7 to make certain that their teens do not act out these frightening beliefs. Because these options are very difficult and painful for the whole family, and relatively ineffective, parents often slide into a middle path. Considering this dilemma, it is essential that you communicate openly and candidly with your children from an early age about not drinking any alcohol—not lecturing, but listening for their self-narrative.

Making sure your teens internalize, maintain, and act on healthy and responsible self-narratives on alcohol in the face of all the contradicting influences is so incredibly daunting you could write a book on it. . . .

The principles that are perhaps most important include, first, to start very early. In this way, your kids are not simply bombarded with your guidance on drinking after they have began to be exposed to it, but rather develop a strong and safe personal-narrative on alcohol from a very young age. Second, don't just say no. Work to find as many other empowering self-narratives to foster and say yes to. That way when your teens' friends tell gushing stories about getting drunk over the weekend and then ask, "What did you do?" they can offer better alternatives, like, "I went mountain climbing with a bunch of really cool people. You should come next time." Finally, don't forget that from the moment of their births you have been your childrens' greatest influence. Drinking around your teens, or allowing them to get started, can be as unwise as smoking around a baby.

"RSDT [random student drug testing]
programs are effective in deterring, reducing and detecting illegal drug use
among students."

# Random Drug Testing Can
# Prevent Student Drug Abuse

## Joseph R. McKinney

*In the following viewpoint Joseph R. McKinney, an adjunct pro-
fessor of law at Ball State University, argues that random student drug testing (RSDT) for participation in extracurricular
activities is necessary to reduce drug use. He analyzes the results
to a follow-up study conducted in the Indiana school system.
Those results reveal that RSDT does not discourage students
from participating in school activities and encourages an overall
decrease in drug use. McKinney asserts that a zero-tolerance
policy is necessary to combat the climbing rates of student drug
abuse.*

As you read, consider the following questions:

1. How much does substance abuse cost the American
   school system each year?

Joseph R. McKinney, "The Effectiveness and Legality of Random Student Drug Testing
Programs Revisited," RandomStudentDrugTesting.org, December 13, 2005. Reproduced
by permission of the author.

2. At the time this viewpoint was written, how many students were using steroids?

3. According to the Office of National Drug Control Policy, what percentage of employers saw a drop in positive drug tests after requiring random drug testing?

It has been three and a half years since the United States Supreme Court broadened the authority of public school officials to use random student drug testing (RSDT) programs to test students for illegal drugs. Increasingly, across the country school districts are adopting RSDT programs as one component of a larger drug awareness and prevention program.

The Supreme Court called the Nation's problem with illegal drug use a "national epidemic." Indeed, recent research on the magnitude and extent of drug use among the Nation's youth indicates the Supreme Court did not overstate the substance-abuse problem. A Columbia University national survey of teens found that 62 percent of high schoolers (9.5 million students) and 28 percent of middle school students (almost 5 million students) report that drugs are used, kept or sold at their schools. Students who attend schools where substances are used, kept and sold are nearly three times more likely to smoke, drink or use illicit drugs as students whose schools are drug-free schools.

Substance abuse adds at least $41 billion dollars each year to the costs of elementary and secondary education in terms of special education, truancy, counseling, teacher turnover, property damage, injury, and other costs. Joseph Califano, President of the National Center on Addiction and Substance Abuse (CASA) [and a former Secretary of Education] said, "Availability is the mother of use. We really are putting an enormous number of 12 to 17 year olds at risk." Looking for help in solving the drug epidemic Califano said, "I think when parents feel as strongly about drugs in the schools as they do about asbestos in the schools, we'll start getting the drugs out of the schools."

Parents probably do not know the extent of drug and alcohol abuse among teenagers. By the time students finish high school 81 percent have drunk alcohol, 47 percent have used marijuana, and (35 percent in the past year) 24 percent have used another illicit drug. Nine and one-half percent have used cocaine within the past year. One million high school students are currently using steroids. The percentage of teens who know a friend or classmate that has abused prescription drugs was up 86 percent in 2005 compared to 2004, from 14 percent to 26 percent.

How should schools and communities deal with the drug problem among America's teenage students? The U.S. Supreme Court found that drug testing students who participate in extracurricular activities is a reasonably effective means of addressing a school district's legitimate interest in preventing, deterring and detecting drug use.

It is difficult to gauge the expansion of random student drug testing (RSDT) programs around the country, but it appears certain that the number of voluntary and mandatory drug testing programs is growing in Texas, New Jersey, Indiana, California, Arkansas, Alaska, Pennsylvania, Oregon, Connecticut, Oklahoma, Mississippi, Florida, Georgia, North Carolina and Kentucky. . . .

## Effectiveness of Random Student Drug Testing Programs

As a follow-up to a 2003 survey of 65 Indiana high schools with random student drug testing programs (RSDT), those same high schools were surveyed again in the spring of 2005 about the effectiveness of RSDT programs. Information on the costs of such programs was incorporated into the most recent survey, along with questions regarding athletic and extracurricular participation levels, along with questions regarding the impact of random student drug programs on student morale. . . .

## Number of School Districts Using RSDT

As of May 2008, it is estimated that a minimum of 16.5% of U.S. school districts have adopted/implemented student random illicit drug testing programs. This represents about 2,000 U.S. school districts. Frequency of adoption/implementation is currently about two districts per week and escalating. This represents a minimum of 1% of school districts per year at the current frequency rate.

*Student Drug-Testing Coalition,*
*"How Many U.S. School Districts Randomly Drug Test Students,"*
*May 2008. www.studentdrugtesting.org.*

The majority of respondents reported that student drug use had *decreased* since their RSDT program began, and that the RSDT programs did not affect student activity participation levels adversely. In fact, almost one-half of principals reported *increases in participation levels for athletic programs.* The reported per-test cost of a RSDT program was $30 or less for 91 percent of the 54 high schools with RSDT programs.

When asked if the RSDT program negatively impacted the classroom, a full 100 percent of principals responding (one respondent left this question blank), stated that they observed no evidence of a negative impact of the prevention program upon the classroom. The majority of testing programs utilized urine specimens and all schools notified parents of test results. The majority of schools temporarily restrict participation in activities upon a positive-test result. Most schools made referrals for some form of counseling when there was a positive test result.

High schools with RSDT programs exceeded the state average for test scores on the state-mandated graduation test as well as exceeding the state average for graduation rates.

*1. Drug use by students (based on written self-reporting surveys):*

- 58% reported that drug use by students decreased

- 42% reported that drug use by students remained the same

- 0% reported that drug use had increased

Eighteen high schools responded that written surveys of student drug use are not utilized.

- 91% of principals stated that they believe that RSDT does, in fact, limit the effects of peer pressure to use drugs.

- 9% of principals stated that they do not believe that RSDT limits peer pressure effects.

- 41% reported that the positive drug-test result rate has decreased.

- 56% reported that the positive drug-test result rate has remained the same.

- 3% reported that the positive drug-test result rate has increased.

*2. Impact of random student drug testing programs:* On athletic program participation:

- 0% of the high schools surveyed reported a reduction in student participation in athletic or extracurricular activities.

- 46% of high schools reported increases in student participation in athletic activities.

- 54% of high schools reported that student participation in athletic activities remained at the same level as before RSDT.

On extracurricular activity participation:

- 45% of high schools reported increases in student participation in extracurricular activities.

- 55% of high schools reported that student participation in extracurricular activities remained at the same level as before RSDT.

On test scores and graduation rates

- 80% (2002–03 school year) and 79% of schools with RSDT achieved scores higher than the state average on the mandated graduation test for grades 10–12;

- 80% of high schools with RSDT programs (2003–04 school year) had more tenth graders passing the two graduation exam standards than the state average;

- 71% (2002–03 school year) and 75% (2003–04 school year) of high schools with RSDT programs had graduation rates higher than the State average.

Impact upon morale

- 100% of principals reported that, despite critics claiming that RSDT has a negative impact in the classroom, their experiences showed this claim to be untrue. . . .

### Covered activities

- 96% test students in athletics

- 78% test students in extracurricular activities

- 72% test students with driving/parking privileges

- 50% test students in co-curricular activities . . .

*Consequences of a positive test result*

- 85% require loss of athletics playing time

- 79% require loss of extracurricular participation time

- 63% require follow-up testing

- 60% require participation in counseling

- 43% require drug education participation . . .

# Getting Drugs Out of Schools

The Supreme Court has spoken and so have several state and federal courts. Random student drug testing is legal with some limitations. The research on RSDT programs also speaks volumes on the effectiveness of drug testing programs. RSDT programs are effective in deterring, reducing and detecting illegal drug use among students. This should not be surprising since drug testing has been effective in the U.S. military and American workplace. The Office of National Drug Control Policy (ONDCP) reports "employers who have followed the federal model [random drug testing] have seen a 67 percent drop in positive drug tests. Along with significant declines in absenteeism, accidents, and health care costs, they've also experienced dramatic increases in worker productivity."

As Joseph Califano, Chairman and President of (CASA) stated, "It's time for parents to shout, 'We're mad as hell and we're not going to take this anymore'! And for education officials in Washington and the states, cities, and counties to mount the same campaign to get drugs out of our schools as they are mounting to increase test scores." One legal and effective means to get the drugs out of schools is RSDT.

*"[Random drug testing is] not associated with a change in the numbers of students who use drugs in any category."*

# Random Drug Testing Cannot Prevent Student Drug Abuse

*Ryan Grim*

*Ryan Grim is a regular contributor to* Slate *magazine and often writes about drug-related issues. In the following viewpoint he discusses the findings of two large-scale studies on the effectiveness of random student drug testing (RSDT). Both studies concluded that RSDT has no impact on student drug use and abuse. He argues that RSDT violates student rights and further funds the multi-million dollar drug-testing industry. Grim asserts that schools should reconsider their drug policies and rely on adult observation as the primary means for determining student drug use.*

As you read, consider the following questions:

1. What did the 2003 Michigan study conclude?

Ryan Grim, "Blowing Smoke," *Slate*, March 21, 2006, pp. 1–5. Copyright © 2006–2008 Washington Post, Newsweek Interactive Co. LLC. All rights reserved. Distributed by United Feature Syndicate, Inc.

2. What did the follow-up Michigan study conclude about marijuana use among 12th graders at schools where students were randomly tested for drugs?

3. How much does the drug-testing industry earn each year?

Drug testing of the American public has been steadily broadening over the past 20 years, from soldiers to grocery baggers to high-school and middle-school students. In its 2007 budget, the Bush administration asks for $15 million to fund random drug testing of students—if approved, a 50 percent increase over 2006. Officials from the federal drug czar's office are crisscrossing the country to sell the testing to school districts.

Yet, according to the two major studies that have been conducted on student testing, it doesn't actually reduce drug use. "Of most importance, drug testing still is found not to be associated with students' reported illicit drug use—even random testing that potentially subjects the entire student body," determined the authors of the most recent study.

It seems like common sense that if students are warned they could be caught getting high any day in school, they'd be less likely to risk it. And principals and the drug czar's office argue that this random chance "gives kids a reason to say no." But teens are notorious for assuming that nothing bad will happen to them. *Sure, some people get caught, but not me.* In addition, a student who chooses to do drugs already has more than a random chance of getting caught—adults are everywhere in this world. Someone could see her, smell smoke, see her bloodshot eyes, or wonder what the hell is so funny. And since most schools test only students who do something more than just show up for class—like join an after-school club, park on campus, or play a sport—kids can avoid the activities rather than quit puffing. Testing may not change much more of the equation than that.

# Study Findings

Such are the findings of two major studies. The first study, published in early 2003, looked at 76,000 students in eighth, 10th, and 12th grades in hundreds of schools, between the years 1998 and 2001. It was conducted by Ryoko Yamaguchi, Lloyd Johnston, and Patrick O'Malley out of the University of Michigan, which also produces *Monitoring the Future*, the university's highly regarded annual survey of student drug use, which is funded by the National Institute on Drug Abuse and whose numbers the White House regularly cites.

The early 2003 Michigan study compared the rates of drug use, as measured by *Monitoring the Future*, in schools that did some type of drug testing to schools that did not. The researchers controlled for various demographic differences and found across the board that drug testing was ineffective; there was no statistically significant difference in the number of users at a school that tested for drugs and a similar school that didn't.

The White House criticized the Michigan study for failing to look at the efficacy of random testing. So, Yamaguchi, Johnston, and O'Malley added the random element and ran their study again, this time adding data for the year 2002. The follow-up study, published later in 2003, tracked 94,000 middle- and high-school students. It reached the same results as its precursor. Even if drug testing is done randomly and without suspicion, it's not associated with a change in the number of students who use drugs in any category. The Michigan follow-up found one exception: In schools that randomly tested students, 12th-graders were *more* likely to smoke marijuana.

Results like these would mean budget cuts or death for some government programs. The White House has devised its own rating system, known as the Program Assessment Rating Tool [PART] to help it cull failed initiatives. In 2002, PART deemed "ineffective" the Safe and Drug Free Schools State

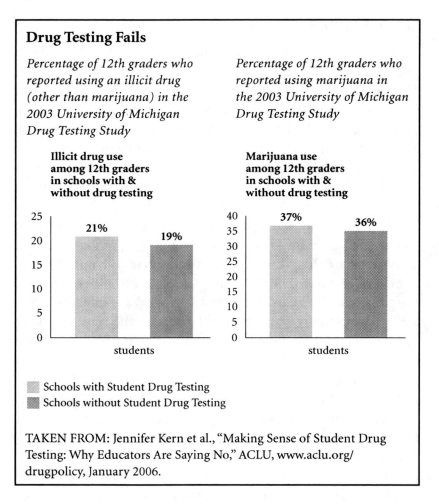

**Drug Testing Fails**

*Percentage of 12th graders who reported using an illicit drug (other than marijuana) in the 2003 University of Michigan Drug Testing Study*

*Percentage of 12th graders who reported using marijuana in the 2003 University of Michigan Drug Testing Study*

**Illicit drug use among 12th graders in schools with & without drug testing**

21%  19%

students

**Marijuana use among 12th graders in schools with & without drug testing**

37%  36%

students

Schools with Student Drug Testing
Schools without Student Drug Testing

TAKEN FROM: Jennifer Kern et al., "Making Sense of Student Drug Testing: Why Educators Are Saying No," ACLU, www.aclu.org/drugpolicy, January 2006.

Grants program, the umbrella for school drug testing. The Office of Management and Budget, which runs the PART evaluations, writes on its Web site, "The program has failed to demonstrate effectiveness in reducing youth drug use, violence, and crime." The PART evaluation did not single out drug testing, which is a small part of the overall state grants program. Still, combined with the Michigan studies, what we have here is a bureaucratic pounding. That hasn't stopped President Bush from sounding an upbeat note. In his 2004 State of the Union, he said, "I proposed new funding to continue our aggressive, community-based strategy to reduce demand for illegal drugs. Drug testing in our schools has proven to be an effective part of this effort."

## Skewed Evidence

Pressed for evidence to support the administration's bid to increase funds for testing, drug officials challenge the Michigan study's methodology. Drug czar John Walters has called for "detailed pre- and post-random testing data"—that is, a study of the rate of drug use at a school before a random testing program was initiated and then again afterward. Such a study is currently under way with federal funds, but it comes with a built-in flaw. Drug-use rates are obtained in questionnaires that school administrators give to students. If the administrators are asking students about their drug-use habits while they have the power to randomly test them, how honest can we expect the students to be, no matter what anonymity they're promised?

Like Walters, the $766 million drug-testing industry isn't ready to give up on testing students, for which it charges between $14 and $30 a cupful of pee. Melissa Moskal, executive director of the 1,300-member Drug and Alcohol Testing Industry Association, pointed me to a preliminary study that she likes better than Michigan's and that Walters also frequently references. The study is funded by the Department of Education and produced by the Institute for Behavior and Health, and its lead author is Robert DuPont, a former White House drug official. DuPont is also a partner at Bensinger, DuPont & Associates [BDA]. DuPont says that Bensinger "doesn't have anything to do with drug testing." But the company's Web site states: "BDA offers a range of products designed to help employers establish and manage workplace drug and alcohol testing programs."

DuPont's study, which he calls "descriptive," chose nine schools that met certain criteria, the first of which was, "The student drug testing program's apparent success." The study's methodology appears to add to the slant. Rather than gathering information from students and analyzing it, DuPont relies on a questionnaire that asks how effective administrators think their random drug-testing program is. He doesn't claim neutrality. "I can't quite get the argument that [drug testing] wouldn't work," he says. He's now working on an evaluation of eight schools. The results won't be ready soon, but let's venture a prediction: Random drug testing will come out looking good.

*"Everything was fine—until more smok-
ers moved in across the hall."*

# Smoking Bans Help Reduce Tobacco Addiction

*Daniel B. Wood*

*During the last few decades, smoking bans have been enacted for
some public buildings, restaurants and bars. Now, as Daniel B.
Wood reports in the following viewpoint, many apartment and
condominium complexes are following suit and creating their
own antismoking policies. Wood, a staff writer for the* Christian
Science Monitor, *finds that seniors are the driving force behind
these policies, since they tend to live in shared facilities and their
health may be more at risk from problems related to smoking.
Apartment and condominium complex owners are also realizing
the benefits to these bans, since they alleviate some of the worry
about safety issues, such as fires, and cleaning units after smokers move out.*

As you read, consider the following questions:

1. What did a 2006 U.S. Surgeon General report reveal
   about secondhand smoke?

Daniel B. Wood, "New No-Smoking Frontier: Condos and Apartments," *Christian Science Monitor*, February 7, 2007. Copyright © 2007 The Christian Science Publishing Society. All rights reserved. Reproduced by permission from *Christian Science Monitor*,
(www.csmonitor.com).

2. How many U.S. public housing commissions are enacting smoking bans each month?
3. Why is the city of Belmont, California, so important regarding apartment and condominium smoking bans?

After retiree Judy Wilson moved from Georgia back to her hometown of Sault Ste. Marie, Mich., in 1997, life was sweet: Fresh air, beautiful scenery, quiet neighbors.

A year later, a heavy smoker moved in across the hall at Ms. Wilson's second-floor apartment in Arlington Town Apartments. Wilson says her life changed.

"I started having all kinds of breathing problems and eye irritations," says Wilson, a retired assembly-line worker. After maintenance personnel tried and failed to stop the smoke in several ways, including ventilation changes, air filters, and intake fans, she was moved to an apartment down the hall. Everything was fine—until more smokers moved in across the hall. "My doctor told me . . . that I'd better move away from it or else," says Wilson.

As similar scenarios play out in apartment and condominium complexes across the country, they are resulting in a new frontier in antismoking policies: private dwellings.

Not only are some condos and apartment houses banning smoking inside private units, but there is talk in Belmont, Calif., of a city law next month [March 2007] that would mandate that all complexes keep a portion of their units smoke-free.

## The Case for Smoking Bans

The war against smoking first ramped up in the 1980s when some of America's public buildings became smoke-free. Then, in the 1990s, a slew of restaurants and bars in US cities banned smoking.

Now, seniors are leading the way in the new battle in part because many live in communal environments and they feel they are susceptible to the health and safety hazards of smoking. "The primary drive for smoke-free housing in America is coming from the elderly," says Jim Bergman, director of the Smoke-Free Environments Law Project in Ann Arbor, Mich.

Smoke-free policies in private dwellings are also taking hold because state and federal laws do not protect smokers in the same way that they protect people from discrimination based on race, ethnicity, and national origin, say experts. But banning a legal behavior in someone's own home is an intrusion of privacy that could set a dangerous precedent that, taken to extremes, could allow government to regulate too much in private life, opponents say.

Smoking can also be safety issue, particularly in close quarters, some say. "There is a great deal of growing interest in the senior housing community about senior smokers because seniors become forgetful and careless about smoking," says Serena Chen, policy director for the American Lung Association of California. Although cigarettes cause 10 percent of apartment fires, 40 percent of apartment fire deaths are attributed to smoking. Such fires cause death because they occur while more people are asleep.

Giving more teeth to the push is a finding in the [June 2006] US Surgeon General report that there are no safe levels of secondhand smoke. [In 2006], the California Air Resources Board declared secondhand smoke to be a toxic air contaminant on par with other industrial pollutants.

## Bans in Condominium and Apartment Complexes

For their part, condo and apartment owners are beginning to realize the additional costs of getting units ready for new tenants after smokers have lived there.

Across the state of Michigan, 12 of 132 housing commissions have banned smoking in multiunit apartments and condos in the [2005 and 2006], Mr. Bergman says. [In 2004], no one could find a smoke-free apartment listing anywhere in the state; now there are more than 5,000, he says.

About two or three public housing commissions in Michigan are adopting smoke-free policies each month; elsewhere in the US, Bergman says, perhaps another one commission per month is doing the same. So far, that means that the public buildings owned and run by such commissions—such as Arlington Courts in Sault Ste. Marie—are taking such actions voluntarily.

But that could change [during March 2007] in California. In Belmont, the city attorney and city council are expected to break new ground by passing a law that affects all public and private apartment and condominium owners in the city, requiring them to adopt smoke-free policies for a certain percentage of their units.

"Belmont will be watched nationally to see how far it goes in requiring apartment owners to have smoke-free policies," says Bergman. "Since no other city has passed a law requiring private apartment owners or condo associations to have a percentage of their units be smoke-free, this will be unique in the nation and other cities will seriously consider taking the step as well."

## The Case Against Smoking Bans

If Belmont's and Michigan's measures are being fueled in part by statistics showing that 80 percent of Americans don't smoke, they are also drawing ire from many among the 20 percent who do. Smokers wonder where they'll be allowed to smoke if new laws proliferate. Even top proponents of smoke-free policies question whether scientific evidence overstates the dangers of being exposed to secondhand smoke, and chases smokers into an ever-shrinking portion of the great outdoors.

"There really is no evidence that even a fleeting whiff of cigarette smoke will give you lung cancer, but that's how proponents of these policies seem to be advancing their cause," says Jacob Sullum, senior editor at *Reason Magazine*, who authored a book about the antismoking movement.

If smokers are banned from apartments and condos, parks, and other public spaces, the only space left for them to smoke will be single-family homes, a place where children reside. "The next angle we are going to see on this is how to protect children from respiratory problems in the home, and that is not the kind of place where I think the government ought to be intervening," says Mr. Sullum.

| "No lives have actually been saved [by smoking bans]."

# Smoking Bans Will Not Reduce Tobacco Addiction

*Joe Jackson*

*In the following viewpoint Joe Jackson, musician and author of several books, including* A Cure for Gravity, *argues that smoking bans have done nothing to protect the health of citizens. He asserts that smoking bans are politically motivated and benefit the antismoking industry. Furthermore, he notes that there is little proof that secondhand smoke is dangerous. Ultimately, according to Jackson, smoking bans will not lead to a reduction in smoking but a loss in profits for businesses like bars and restaurants.*

As you read, consider the following questions:

1. When was the smoking ban introduced in New York City?

2. According to the author, what is the only justifiable reason for a smoking ban?

3. In what year was the tobacco industry first banned from stating that smoking was safe?

So: an anti-smoking fanatic is elected Mayor of New York and passes a ban on smoking in every bar, restaurant and nightclub, claiming that 'secondhand smoke' has killed more New Yorkers in the last two years than the catastrophe of Sept. 11th [2001 terrorist attacks]! He further exploits that tragedy by claiming (and this has been dutifully repeated in the media) that 'the hospitality industry is doing *better* since the ban was passed'. But the ban was introduced in mid-2003, when *the whole city economy* was starting to recover from the huge post-9/11 slump. Then, to cook the books still further, Mayor Bloomberg includes in 'the hospitality industry' hotels, restaurants (which were already non-smoking except in separate bar areas, an arrangement which was working pretty well), fast-food outlets, Starbucks, and even liquor stores. So, if McDonalds hires a couple of thousand new employees, or if more people buy booze to take home because they can't smoke in a bar—it all supposedly demonstrates the success of the smoking ban!

Meanwhile anyone who actually goes to NY [New York] bars and clubs knows that the ban is extremely unpopular and causing all kinds of problems, 'bad vibes', and significant loss of trade. (Why would the Empire State Restaurant and Tavern Association be suing the city if business were booming?!) Employees (whom the ban is supposed to 'protect') hate having to be cops, and for less tips, at that. Some lose their jobs as smaller bars go out of business. Even jukebox companies are protesting, because people are standing out on the street smoking instead of feeding their machines! Many bars defy the law and let people smoke, but they all have to display a notice with a phone number to call 'to report violations.' In other words, to 'rat on' your neighbours.

What has the ban really achieved, except lost business, anger, confusion and social tension? No lives have actually been saved, and people who simply don't like smoke could have been accommodated by (a) good air-cleaning systems and (b) a market-driven *choice* of smoking and non-smoking spaces. (If there's so much popular demand for a ban, why did it need to be enforced by law in the first place? And why did Bloomberg wait until after he was elected before even proposing it?)

It is important to make this distinction: the 'nuisance factor' of smoke, to those who dislike it, *is a separate issue*. It is not a health or safety issue concerning doctors or politicians, but a service issue, mostly concerning the hospitality industry. The only real justification for a total legal ban would be *incontrovertible proof that S H S [secondhand smoke] is a deadly health hazard*. If that is ever anywhere *near* proven, I will give up smoking immediately, law or no law, since I am not a murderer. Besides, if we're going to accept such low thresholds of risk as a basis for public policy, we should certainly ban workers from kitchens (since cooking food produces carcinogens) and also ban *music*, since it is well-established that loud music damages peoples' hearing. What about bartenders in dance clubs?

Incidentally, since the 'strongest' evidence of S H S risk comes from 'spousal' studies, there is a stronger case for banning smoke in the home than in a bar. The fact that there is no effort (yet) to do so suggests a respect for property rights. But publicans, restaurateurs and nightclub owners have property rights too. Their establishments are not funded by taxes, nor is anyone actually compelled to enter. They have as much right to set their own smoking policy as you do in your own living room.

## Arguments in Favor of Smoking Bans

A couple of other arguments for smoking bans need to be briefly addressed. One is that 'smokers are the minority.' True enough: about 26% of Britons, for example, are reckoned to smoke. But in pubs this goes up to around 50%, and in some pubs it's quite apparent that smokers are the majority. Also, when it comes to nightlife, *non* smokers are not necessarily *anti* smokers; in fact they mostly don't mind smoke as long as there isn't too much of it. So blanket smoking bans in bars and clubs are *not* demanded by a majority of the people who go to them (and if they were, why was there not even *one* non-smoking bar in New York before the ban?) But ultimately, percentages are not the point. The Hospitality Industry is, by definition, meant to be welcoming and inclusive. That's why there are meatless dishes on the menu, bottles of Pernod [an anise-flavored liqueur] behind the bar even though hardly anyone ever drinks it, etc etc. Even if smokers were only 5%, that alone does not justify throwing them out onto the street.

It is disingenuous, too, to say that smokers are not being barred from the bar, but just barred from smoking. This is like telling a vegetarian that his favourite restaurant has been turned into a steakhouse but he's still welcome! For many of us, a drink and a smoke complement each other so perfectly that being forbidden to smoke is not only infuriating but a genuine loss, the loss of a cherished pleasure and a part of our lifestyle. One smoker I know describes it as 'like being forced to eat chips with no salt'.

To say that smoking bans in 'public places' (including, let's not forget, *private property* like bars and clubs) are justified in order to get more smokers to quit is equally wrongheaded. For one thing, it is social engineering; an inappropriate politicisation of a personal decision. It is also ineffectual as long as smoking remains legal, since the most determined and addictive smokers (the ones who really 'should' quit) will simply smoke more elsewhere. Often they smoke more than ever, out of sheer defiance. Again and again, doctors and politicians fail to understand that *pleasure and free choice are just as important to people as 'health'*; in fact, they are *part* of 'health'. De-

"He says the workplace smoking ban doesn't apply to him as he's not intending to do any work." Cartoon by Fran. www.CartoonStock.com.

priving people of their pleasures makes them unhappy. Nagging, bullying and coercing them makes them angry and rebellious as well.

Still another spurious argument is that smoking bans are justified so that no one's clothes or hair will ever have to smell of smoke. This complaint is sometimes heard from bartenders who feel for some reason that they should be exempted from the millions of people who have to take a shower and change their clothes after work. Once again, this can be mostly resolved by more choice and good air-cleaning sytems (about which more in a moment). And if there are still some occasions when the air gets smokier than it should, is a bit of give-and-take on the part of non-smokers really too much to ask?

No doubt it must be pleasant for someone who dislikes smoke to know that he or she can go anywhere, any time, and never be bothered by the slightest whiff. Personally, I'd feel more comfortable if dogs were universally banned, because I'm allergic to them. But I like to think I see the bigger picture, and if anyone proposed a dog ban, I would oppose it. I ask non-smokers to consider this: you don't have to deal with smoke in your home, your office, your car, in shops, schools, cinemas, theatres, planes or trains. But tobacco is still *legal.* How in a free-market democracy, can you say that we can never, at any time or in any place, enjoy it in a social setting? If the anti-smokers are right about S H S, we should not smoke at home either (unless we live alone) so as not to endanger our family members. So if smoking is banned in every bar—and even in private clubs—where *can* we smoke? Only on street corners, which—as the anti-smokers are well aware—makes us feel bad and *look* bad. And then we're in trouble for making noise or leaving fag-ends [cigarette butts] on the pavement! Some cities are even proposing to ban smokers from certain main streets, so that children will not be corrupted by the sight of us. Why not go all the way and put us in the stocks, to be pelted with garbage?!

This is Prohibition in all but name. At least Prohibition was honest and unequivocal. The crusade against tobacco attempts instead to make life so miserable for smokers that we will all eventually give up 'of our own accord.' But tobacco can't be 'un-invented,' and there will always be many people who enjoy it. Smokers are not going to go away. If tobacco were prohibited by law, you'd have all sorts of other problems—illegal trafficking, etc. Besides, there isn't a government in the world which wants to give up the enormous tax revenues they get from tobacco. Sooner or later, the pendulum will have to swing back towards accommodating smokers by a sensible mix of free choice, tolerance, and technology. And the best venues for smoking will always be well-ventilated pubs, clubs, bars, and restaurants (or at least some restaurants or parts of restaurants). At the same time, if there's a genuine demand for more completely non-smoking venues, the free market will sort it out. . . .

## Health, Politics, or Profit?

The more I investigate the 'tobacco wars,' the more obvious it becomes that this is not so much a health issue as a political one. The much-demonised tobacco companies made some big mistakes in the 1960s–1980s and fell out of favour. The whole story is a bit beyond the scope of this essay, but briefly, they reacted to revelations that smoking was riskier than previously believed by going into 'denial mode', which then enabled their opponents to inflate the dangers of smoking more and more. Then came the lawsuits, and they started to go from denial to capitulation. They are now widely banned from advertising and in the US, since 1998, even banned from presenting any evidence which would contradict the anti-smoking orthodoxy (in exchange for immunity from further lawsuits). Anti-smokers keep portraying the tobacco industry as an insidiously influential 'evil empire,' and anyone who's even remotely pro-smoking as a tobacco industry stooge. But in reality, that industry has been largely silenced. Tobacco companies are mostly keeping quiet and contenting themselves with expanding markets in China, Eastern Europe, etc. Many smokers are angry at tobacco companies for 'selling us out'. The Philip

Morris Web site, for instance, should get some kind of award for corporate masochism; looking at it, I thought I'd wandered into an anti-smoking Web site by mistake. But they're saying what they have to say in order to stay in business. I agree with anti-smokers that a corporation like Philip Morris is fundamentally cynical and concerned with making money, rather than health or any kind of moral principle. What I don't see, though, is how this makes them any different to McDonalds, or Coca Cola, or GlaxoSmithKline, or Enron, or Halliburton.

Lo and behold, since 1998 we've seen a huge increase in *unopposed* anti-smoking propaganda, and also in advertising for 'smoking replacement' products: the nicotine patch, gum, etc. And it doesn't take a lot of digging to discover that big pharmaceutical companies are the biggest contributors to the anti-smoking crusade. The Robert Wood Johnson (of Johnson & Johnson) Foundation alone has contributed *over half a billion dollars* to anti-smoking campaigns, including even many small 'grass-roots' ones which lobby legislators. They and other drug companies reap the benefits by selling 'politically correct' nicotine. Typically, though, these products don't work very well, and smokers go on and off them, sometimes for years, spending a lot of money in the process.

# Periodical Bibliography

*The following articles have been selected to supplement the diverse views presented in this chapter.*

| | |
|---|---|
| Sarah Baldauf | "Protective Measures," *U.S. News and World Report*, March 17, 2008. |
| Lauren Cahoon | "Impulsivity Linked to Cocaine Addiction," *Science Now*, June 6, 2008. |
| Diane Cole | "Quit It," *National Geographic*, January 2008. |
| Joseph DiFranza | "Hooked from the First Cigarette," *Scientific American*, May 2008. |
| Cynthia Geppert | "Between Pain and Addiction," *Psychiatric Times*, October 2007. |
| Arline Kaplan | "Risk of Substance Abuse Not Increased by ADHD Drugs," *Psychiatric Times*, July 2008. |
| Peter Lake | "Four Approaches to Prevention and the Law," *Student Affairs Leader*, August 1, 2007. |
| Kyle Morrison | "Prescription for a Deadly Addiction," *Safety and Health*, June 2008. |
| Fred Reed | "Dangerous Addiction," *American Conservative*, October 6, 2008. |
| Nora Schultz | "Smoking Gene Protects Against Cocaine Addiction," *New Scientist*, June 21, 2008. |
| Rebecca Wearn | "The Drugs Don't Work," *New Internationalist*, August 2008. |

# How Do Addictions Affect Relationships?

# Chapter Preface

In 1998 the Medical University of South Carolina began secretly testing pregnant women for drug use. Once found positive, these women were referred to drug counseling. If the women tested positive for drugs a second time, they were arrested and charged with various crimes depending on their term of pregnancy. Ten of these women decided to pursue legal action against the hospital based on what they believed to be a violation of the Fourth Amendment, which guarantees freedom from unwarranted search and seizure. In *Ferguson v. City of Charleston*, the Supreme Court ruled in favor of the women. The controversy over this case led many Americans to question the role of law in the lives of pregnant women.

Some people, like the staff members of the Medical University of South Carolina, argue that it is society's responsibility to ensure that children, including unborn children, are protected from harm. Citing the importance of fetal rights, more than twenty states have enacted laws that can punish women for dangerous behaviors during pregnancy. Consequences for alcohol and drug use while pregnant can lead to charges of child abuse, contributing to the delinquency of a minor (through the umbilical cord), and even attempted murder. Although no state has established laws that make any particular behavior during pregnancy illegal, a 2000 report by the Center for Reproductive Rights found that more than 200 pregnant women across the country have been arrested or prosecuted under current child abuse laws.

Not everyone supports such actions. The Drug Policy Alliance (DPA) argues that arresting pregnant women for drug and alcohol abuse does not encourage women to get treatment for substance abuse and that it does not help promote the overall health of women and their unborn babies. The DPA notes, "The threat of criminal punishment fosters a climate of fear and mistrust between doctors and patients, imperiling the health both of women and their future children." It is for this reason that leading public health organizations such as the American Academy of Pediatrics and the American Medical Association oppose policing pregnant women and their behaviors. Complicating the issue is the lack of drug treatment programs designed for pregnant women.

According to the Guttmacher Institute, "For many lawmakers, the issue comes down to the difficult task of balancing a woman's right to bodily integrity with society's interest in ensuring healthy pregnancies, and the question of whether punitive approaches will foster—or hinder—healthy outcomes for women and children." Ultimately, like the authors in this chapter, all parties involved are concerned for the health and well-being of mothers and babies. Determining how to help pregnant women who abuse drugs and alcohol will continue to be a struggle as long as society walks the thin line between mother's rights and fetal rights.

*"I don't see the BlackBerry as being an 'issue' in my life."*

# Increasing Dependence on Online Communication Helps Relationships

*Rae Hoffman*

*Rae Hoffman is the editorial director of BBGeeks.com, a Web site devoted to BlackBerry users. In the following viewpoint, she argues that while BlackBerry use can become problematic, even addictive, it can actually be beneficial for relationships. Because Hoffman is able to be reached for work purposes at any time through her BlackBerry, she can participate in activities with her family that she might otherwise have to miss out on. She can spend time with her children and attend school functions because she does not have to be at the office as often because of her BlackBerry.*

As you read, consider the following questions:

1. Why have BlackBerries been nicknamed CrackBerries?

2. What percentage of employees from a company studied felt that they were somewhat compulsive about their BlackBerry use?

3. Under what circumstances has the author's BlackBerry use alienated others?

A few weeks ago, I noticed that Chris Butler [vice president of New Fangled Web Factory] had done a post asking if the BlackBerry rules your life via our Twitter feed. I then saw a post this week [January 2008] about how your BlackBerry can't love you back that was referencing a post we did this summer about heightening BlackBerry addiction. And I think all of us have seen an article or two about how the BlackBerry is becoming commonplace—maybe too commonplace—and for some, at a price in their personal lives.

## Signs of Addiction

Some of the below were ones that resonated with me for various reasons:

> Blackberry e-mail devices can be so addictive that owners may need to be weaned off them with treatment similar to that given to drug users, experts warned today. They said the palmtop gadgets, which have been nicknamed 'crackberries' because users quickly become hooked on them, could be seriously damaging to mental health.

I'm definitely addicted to my BlackBerry according to "society standards" I check it many, many times throughout the day. I've experienced the phantom ringtone (though for me, it is more like a phantom vibration) more times than I can count. I never forget it, and the less than a handful amount of times I've had, I've turned around to go home and retrieve it—even if it meant being late to the place I'm headed.

> Ninety percent of individuals at the company studied said they felt some degree of compulsion in their BlackBerry use. They check their messages not only on evenings and weekends, but also at church, at the gym, at the doctor's office

and even at social gatherings. All this despite the fact that their company doesn't require them to be on call.

I admit to taking my BlackBerry everywhere at all times. I've checked it on the treadmill at the gym. I always have it at social gatherings. I hook the thing to my pajama pants on the weekend mornings. It is the first thing I put on and the last thing I take off on a daily basis. My friends joke that you can spot pictures of me with my face cut off if my "BlackBerry hip" is showing. There is only one time when my BlackBerry is ignored and I'm going to have to let you guess when that is.

And while my company doesn't require me to be on call, I feel the need to be since I am the CEO even though I'm sure the company wouldn't explode if I didn't get every single e-mail instantaneously.

There is a new member of the family, and, like all new siblings, this one is getting a disproportionate amount of attention, resulting in jealousy, tantrums, even trips to the therapist. It's the BlackBerry.

This article was the one that definitely made me think about the issue the hardest. I have children. And I will fully admit to my three-year-old having a fake cell phone clipped to his hip that he called a "BwackBerry" once or twice in his life. I've stood outside my daughter's school e-mailing on the BlackBerry while waiting for her to be released. I've taken it with me to school functions. My kids have grown up in a BlackBerry household and I'd bet they don't remember a time without it.

## Not a Major Problem

Reading these articles, I am this "victim" (and in some opinions, have made my children victims) of all the above Black-Berry harm on my life. But, here's the thing . . . I don't see the BlackBerry as being an "issue" in my life. I'm sure some people will argue, but all I can do is give you my, non-researcher, devout BlackBerry user side of things.

The first thing I should point out is that my significant other in life is also a devout BB [BlackBerry] user. He uses it as frequently as I do and you'd be hard pressed to find either of us in the house at any point in time without the Black-Berry within reaching distance. So, I don't have a resentful partner seething every time I pick the thing up. In all honesty, we're both glad to have a partner who understands and allows our attachment to the device. Sure, there are ground rules and some times that are off limits (we wouldn't start texting on messenger while arguing for instance—we are *sane*) but for the most part, 98 percent BlackBerry infiltration is accepted. Additionally, we talk on messenger throughout the day—so the BlackBerry actually allows us to have *more* contact with each other than we would without it.

Additionally, I work in the Internet sector as do most of my friends. Almost everyone I know and see on a daily basis is attached to the Web remotely—be it via a BlackBerry, Treo or other smartphone. Myself and two friends will go to lunch with all of us checking our BlackBerries randomly throughout the meal. Friends without smartphones are so used to a large percentage of us having them that they see their presence in everyday activities as "normal".

We all utilize our BlackBerries not only as business tools, but also to speak with each other on BlackBerry messenger, to communicate with each other through Facebook, via SMS for those without smartphones . . . you get the picture.

## Alienating Others

That said, I'd be lying if I said there hadn't been times that the BlackBerry has alienated people. I visited a friend last year and upon arriving home, he informed me that his wife had mentioned I had been quite rude throughout the trip. I was utterly confused and then he told me it was because I was "always on the BlackBerry". He explained that while he was used

## What Is a BlackBerry?

BlackBerry is a handheld device made by RIM (Research In Motion) that is marketed primarily for its wireless e-mail handling capability. Through partners, BlackBerry also provides access to other Internet services. Like the Palm, BlackBerry is also a personal digital assistant (PDA) that can include software for maintaining a built-in address book and personal schedule. In addition, it can also be configured for use as a pager.

*"What Is BlackBerry?" Whatis.com, 2008.*

to it after years of being friends with me, his wife was not and thought the constant checking of my BlackBerry was rude.

Being surrounded by BB acceptance the way that I am has indeed created a much higher "acceptable use" threshold in my day to day life than the general world will tolerate. As a result, I try to limit my BlackBerry usage when in those "non-techie" circles, though it is still with me and still checked. Just not while someone is talking to me or I'm at a dinner table.

As far as my children go, I can't say for sure what goes on in their minds. What I can say is that a BlackBerry is an appliance that has been present in their lives as far back as they can remember. Like a computer, or television—the BlackBerry has always been in our household. Granted, the BlackBerry is also attached to my hip, but much like a child of a career military soldier adapts to moving around a lot, kids can also adapt to the presence of electronic devices—especially when they've been present all their lives.

My children also know that the BlackBerry allows me to do things I otherwise wouldn't be able to do. I can attend field trips during the day because I can deal with business related issues from the road if they come up. We can go to a movie on the night of an important technical upgrade because if something happens, I can be reached. And the reason my children have what they have in life is because of my dedication to work—which includes being available whenever the need arises. But instead of being at my office until 8 p.m. on hectic nights, I'm at home, on the couch, watching TV with them. Yes, my BlackBerry needs to be within reach . . . but I can't help think it is better to have me at home with a BlackBerry then have me at the office without one.

I don't see a severely detrimental issue with my BlackBerry usage—even though my usage of it is at "addiction levels" based on the opinions in the above articles. It causes no strife in my relationship with my significant other, it has not caused any issue that has been verbalized by my children at home and allows me to have the best of both worlds. And in the end, that is what technology is supposed to make it easier to do, right?

> "[Constant personal digital assistant use] often results in fatigue, a lack of intimacy, resentment, increased conflict and even premature career burnout."

# Increasing Dependence on Online Communication Hurts Relationships

### Diane K. Danielson

*Diane K. Danielson is the CEO and founder of the Downtown Women's Club, a women's networking organization, and the author of several books, including* The Savvy Gal's Guide to Online Networking. *In the following viewpoint she argues that BlackBerries and other portable communication devices are wreaking havoc on relationships. She cites several examples of how being available 24 hours a day can lead to less intimacy and an overall lack of interest in romantic partners. Ultimately, Danielson asserts that people must learn how to limit their use of these devices.*

As you read, consider the following questions:

1. What did the March 2005 Families and Work Institute study conclude?

2. What are DINS?

3. What did the Kinsey Institute conclude about sex in its 2003 study?

"My husband and I are definitely 'CrackBerry' addicts. We are a sight, staggering out of bed in the morning, reaching for the BlackBerry before even going to the bathroom," says Kellie Appel, a senior vice president and general manager for Turner Trade Group. She and her attorney husband have fast-paced careers, two young children and a dependency on technology to keep everything in sync.

To some, like Appel, wireless devices are a necessity. They allow flexibility where previously there was none, the ability to travel extensively for work and a means to keep up with our global economy. Still, even those most reliant on this technology have concerns about never ending workweeks and constant interruptions impacting personal relationships.

Kristine Robak, a sales director at Suez Energy Resources North America in Boston, manages $100 million in energy contracts and has resisted adopting a BlackBerry. She already suffers through her project manager husband's checking e-mails during mealtimes, even while speeding down highways. However, a recent promotion means more travel for Robak, and her company is ready to order her one of the devices. The question she mulls over is that while it might be practical for work and for the flexibility her 1-year-old son requires, is it also good for her marriage?

Married couples are not the only ones being affected by the home invasion of wireless technology. Ask any upwardly mobile single and they'll tell you that they're often too busy getting ahead in the boardroom to get busy in the bedroom. "Unfortunately, technology is the modern-day equivalent to the spinster chaperone," says Lisa Daily, author of *Stop Getting Dumped! All You Need to Know to Make Men Fall Madly in Love with You and Marry "The One" in 3 Years Or Less.*

"Once you finally manage to squeeze in a romantic dinner and maybe a meaningful conversation, our technological umbilical cord to the office starts buzzing away and the mood—and maybe the opportunity—is lost."

Patricia A. Farrell, Ph.D., an Englewood, N.J.-based clinical psychologist and author of *How to Be Your Own Therapist: A Step-by-Step Guide to Taking Back Your Life*, often treats couples for whom work comes first at the expense of their relationships. "Time seems to be allocated for so much work and work-related activity that relationships are suffering," Farrell says. "When couples are free from [work], often they have a feeling of guilt because they [think they] should be doing something other than relaxing and enjoying each other's company."

Enter the BlackBerry. Faced with an increasing workload, Americans are relying more and more on personal digital assistants (PDAs) with e-mail access such as the BlackBerry, Palm's Treo, Motorola's Q-Phone and soon, Apple's iPhone. But surveys show we're not using these devices to reign in our work hours; instead we're adopting technology to help us work harder, faster and longer.

## Too Busy for Sex

Despite its appeal as the ultimate life/work balance tool, the PDA—like its predecessors the cell phone and pager—may in fact be increasing our stress by opening up around-the-clock access to and from the workplace. In March 2005, the Families and Work Institute released its study "Overwork in America: When the Way We Work Becomes Too Much," which found that employees in contact with work outside of normal work hours are more often highly overworked than those with little or no contact.

What does this mean for constantly connected couples? According to therapists and psychologists, around-the-clock access to the office often results in fatigue, a lack of intimacy, resentment, increased conflict and even premature career burnout. All of which are enough to crater a less-than-solid marriage or relationship. Robert Reich, the former U.S. secretary of labor, popularized the term "DINS couples" (double income, no sex) when he discussed the hazards of work overload in a 2001 speech. While the comment drew laughs, it also brought to light a developing problem: People are working too much to have sex. In 2003, the Kinsey Institute reported that today's women are having much less sex than their 1950s counterparts.

This rings true for Appel and her hard-working female colleagues, who find themselves reminding each other to find the time and energy for sex with their partners. But despite their best efforts and their PDA-enabled scheduling capabilities, it seems that everyone is still too busy and, most of all, too tired.

Psychologist Debra Mandel, Ph.D., is not surprised. She's observed the increase in DINS couples firsthand. "They're not having sex because there's no time," says Mandel, author of *Healing the Sensitive Heart: How to Stop Getting Hurt, Build Your Inner Strength, and Find the Love You Deserve.* "Couples today are burnt-out and exhausted." Tina B. Tessina, Ph.D., a psychotherapist and co-author of *How to Be a Couple and Still Be Free*, agrees. "I think it's a common problem today, and it's growing bigger," Tessina says. Both suspect that wireless technology is adding to the problem, and, according to Tessina, "If there are underlying tensions in the marriage, [being constantly connected to the office] will exacerbate them."

## Avoiding Intimacy

While wireless technology can keep you connected to the office, PDAs are less effective in helping busy executives schedule time for their personal lives, according to Fiona Travis, Ph.D., an Ohio-based psychologist and author of *Should You Marry a Lawyer? A Couple's Guide to Balancing Work, Love and*

*Ambition.* "Those who think that the PDA helps them find time are really fooling themselves; it is just another way of avoiding being intimate," Travis says. This lack of intimacy is all too often the byproduct of our increasing thirst for instant gratification. Mandel, based in Encino, Calif., believes our constant connectivity eliminates our ability to appreciate downtime. "We are losing leisure and downtime where we are not being bombarded by stimuli all the time," Mandel says. "In the old days, we could go out to dinner and be more aware of our surroundings. Now that creates boredom, and people want to fill in the gaps."

Across the city in Long Beach, Tessina sees the desire for "nanosecond communication" as having ramifications everywhere. "People are now expecting instant relationships as well as all other kinds of instant gratification," she says. "The speed of communication may help us get more done, but it doesn't necessarily enhance the quality of life." Tessina believes that too much PDA use results in insufficient real contact, leaving us feeling overloaded and longing to be left alone.

In a dark twist, our thirst for instant gratification and the lack of intimacy at home may, in some cases, lead to more sex outside the home. Alex Halavais, assistant professor of communication and the graduate director of informatics at the University at Buffalo, studies the move from mass society to network society and says that the drive for instant gratification in the area of sex and pornography often drives technology. He points to *Playboy* as being at the forefront of downloading content to cellphones.

## A Third Person in the Bedroom

"In my first marriage, I used to schlep home two briefcases of paperwork . . . and spread them out over the bed, working until 12:30 a.m. while my husband slept," confesses Debra A. Dinnocenzo, president of ALLearnatives, a Pittsburgh provider of learning resources for people in the virtual workplace. Dinnocenzo is also co-author of *Dot Calm: The Search for Sanity in a Wired World* and tells this story specifically to illustrate that technology doesn't make people work more hours; people make people work more hours. Now in her second marriage, Dinnocenzo is much more conscious about the downsides of bringing work home. She recognizes that "technology makes it easy for workaholics to facilitate those tendencies." She stopped bringing home the reams of paper but admits bringing a BlackBerry to bed is not much different.

Sociologist Phyllis Moen at the University of Minnesota is also wary about bringing wireless technology into the bedroom. In her research on the changing nature of careers and the experiences of dual-earner couples, Moen, co-author of *The Career Mystique: Cracks in the American Dream* and editor of *It's About Time: Couples and Careers*, interviewed one individual who likened his working on his laptop in bed at night to "having a third person in the bedroom." Today, if you bring a BlackBerry to bed you might as well be sleeping with your entire address book (and a few random spammers).

Do the dynamics change depending upon whether one or both members in a relationship snuggle up with their wireless devices? Mandel says yes: "The one who is less connected [can have] a lot of resentment and have a hard time seeing the pros of [wireless technology]." Farrell agrees. "When only one is connected constantly, it can be a source of irritation," she says. However, she also sees double the problem when you double the devices, as it could lead to a disconnect where work takes precedence over personal needs or the relationship. "When two are being pulled by the pressures of work, even in their at-home time, the relationship can begin to wear thin and dissolving it becomes an increasingly viable option."

But even completely wired individuals agree the one all important secret is to know when to hit the off button. Alexandra Lebenthal, president of Lebenthal & Co., a New York City-based financial services firm, and mother of three, received her wake-up call last summer at the end of her maternity leave (which she credits her BlackBerry for making possible). It was around 5 p.m. on the Friday of Labor Day weekend and she was vacationing with her family at the beach on Long Island. Hopping off a motorboat onto the dock, she whipped out her BlackBerry from her shorts pocket, only to have it slip through her fingers and sink into the depths of Great South Bay. After an initial scream of shock and despair, she had to laugh. She knew it was a sign that on the Friday evening of a long weekend, there's nobody who needs to connect with you more than your loved ones. She and others are learning: Control your connectivity—or be controlled by it.

*"Pornography turns people into com-
modities."*

# Pornography Addiction
# Can Lead to
# Violence Against Women

*Daniel Weiss*

*In the following viewpoint Daniel Weiss asserts that addiction to
pornography leads to violence against women and children. He
advanced his argument at the Summit on Pornography and Violence Against Women and Children, an annual conference held
in Washington, DC. He notes that as rates of pornography addiction have increased so have incidences of sexual crimes. Furthermore, Weiss claims that pornography presents a threat to the
overall well-being of citizens because it depicts people as objects.*

As you read, consider the following questions:

1. According to Dr. Patrick Carnes, approximately how
   many people are sexually addicted?

2. In 2001 what percentage of sex offenders in Utah were
   adolescents?

"Pornography: Harmless Fun or Public Health Hazard," taken from speech made by
Daniel Weiss on May 19, 2005, and reprinted on the Focus on the Family Web site
(www.family.org/socialissues). Copyright © 2005 Focus on the Family. All rights reserved. International copyright secured. Used by permission.

3. According to the FBI, what is the most common interest among serial killers?

Good morning. I appreciate the opportunity to participate in this forum. My name is Daniel Weiss and I serve as Focus on the Family's Senior Analyst for Media and Sexuality. As we consider pornography and the law, we must answer a foundational question: Does the state have a compelling interest in protecting people from obscene materials?

Folks on this panel may agree that the state does have such an interest, but U.S. District Judge Gary Lancaster came to a different conclusion in 2005. Dismissing the Justice Department's case against Extreme Associates, a company producing rape and torture films, Lancaster wrote that "the government can no longer rely on the advancement of a moral code . . . as a legitimate, let alone a compelling state interest."

Aside from ignoring clear Supreme Court precedent, Lancaster's ruling recognized no harm posed by obscene materials. However this case is ultimately decided, it underscores a declining lack of recognition in legal and cultural realms of pornography's threats to individuals, families, and society.

Ultimately, for obscenity law to be consistently and effectively enforced, our culture must understand the facts on pornography.

## Pornography Facts

More than 25 years ago, Dr. Victor Cline identified the progressive nature of pornography addiction. Once addicted, a person's need for pornography escalates both in frequency and in deviancy. The person then grows desensitized to the material, no longer getting a thrill from what was once exciting. Finally, this escalation and desensitization drives many addicts to act out their fantasies on others.

At a Senate hearing in 2004, medical experts corroborated Cline's breakthroughs. New technology is allowing doctors to look inside addicts' brains to determine just how damaging pornography is. The witnesses described research showing the similarity of porn addiction to cocaine addiction. Further, because images are stored in the brain and can be recalled at any moment, these experts believe that a porn addiction may be harder to break than a heroin addiction.

No one is seriously advocating the legalization of cocaine or heroin, but somehow the pornography industry has convinced a large segment of the population that viewing porn is not only harmless fun, but is also a fundamental right.

By not calling pornography what it is—highly addictive and destructive—we are heading for troubled times. Dr. Patrick Carnes, a leading researcher on sex addiction, estimates that 3 to 6 percent of Americans are sexually addicted. That's as many as 20 million people.

## Effects on Families and Children

This epidemic isn't confined to individuals. Pornography is one of the leading causes of family breakdown today. Two-thirds of the divorce attorneys attending a 2002 meeting of the American Academy of Matrimonial Lawyers said excessive interest in online porn contributed to more than half of the divorces they handled that year. They also said pornography had an almost nonexistent role in divorce just seven or eight years earlier.

An informal poll conducted through Focus on the Family's Web site found that 50 percent of more than 50,000 respondents said they had been negatively affected by pornography.

This devastation isn't confined to adults, either. The Justice Department estimates that nine of 10 children between the ages of 8 and 16 have been exposed to pornography online. Software company Symantec found that 47 percent of school-age children receive pornographic spam on a daily basis, and representatives from the pornography industry told

## Internet Pornography Statistics

| | |
|---|---|
| Pornographic websites | 4.2 million (12% of total websites) |
| Pornographic pages | 420 million |
| Daily pornographic search engine requests | 68 million (25% of total search engine requests) |
| Daily pornographic emails | 2.5 billion (8% of total emails) |
| Internet users who view porn | 42.7% |
| Received unwanted exposure to sexual material | 34% |
| Average daily pornographic emails/user | 4.5 per Internet user |
| Monthly pornographic downloads (peer-to-peer) | 1.5 billion (35% of all downloads) |
| Websites offering illegal child pornography | 100,000 |
| Sexual solicitations of youth made in chat rooms | 89% |
| Youths who received sexual solicitation | 1 in 7 (down from 2003 stat of 1 in 3) |
| Worldwide visitors to pornographic web sites | 72 million visitors to pornography: monthly |
| Internet pornography sales | $4.9 billion |

TAKEN FROM: Family Safe Media, "Pornography Statistics," www.familysafemedia.com, 2008.

Congress that as much as 20 to 30 percent of the traffic to some pornographic Web sites is children.

Ralph DiClemente, a behavioral scientist at Emory University, described the danger of this exposure. He said, "[Children] can't just put [porn] into their worldview, because they don't have one." He went on to explain that pornography becomes a building block in a child's mental and emotional development.

When pornography becomes a filter through which the rest of life is understood, serious damage occurs. A 2001 report found that more than half of all sex offenders in Utah are adolescents—and children as young as 8 years old are committing felony sexual assault.

The porn industry fights laws such as the Child Online Protection Act, which requires pornographers to use age-verification systems, because they know this flood of pornographic imagery is creating a new generation of consumers.

## Pornography and Sexual Violence

This culture-wide hyper-sexualization is generating incredible public health risks. One in five adults in the United States has a sexually transmitted infection (STI), and 19 million new STIs occur annually, almost half of them among youths aged 15 to 24.

Pornography is also a significant factor in sexual violence. The FBI reports that the most common interest among serial killers is hardcore pornography. Another report found that 87 percent of child molesters studied were regular consumers of hardcore pornography. In the spring of 2005, the nation mourned 8-year-old Jessica DeLaTorre, who was abducted, raped and murdered by a porn addict who had viewed child pornography at an Internet café the night before.

Many may also recall Ted Bundy, the serial killer from Florida. In an interview with Focus on the Family founder Dr. James Dobson just hours before he was executed, Bundy described how early exposure to pornography consumed him and led him down his murderous path. He said he was ultimately responsible for his actions, but that the messages in pornography primed him for those actions.

As horrifying as this is, we should not be surprised. Although the Supreme Court was clear in *Miller v. California* that hard-core pornography enjoys no First Amendment protection, lax federal and state law enforcement has essentially given obscenity the protection denied to it in the Constitution.

This lack of enforcement has allowed a back-alley enterprise to grow into an unprecedented global trade in humans. Pornography turns people into commodities. Men and women become sexual objects to be bought, sold, used and discarded. The last time the United States recognized human beings as consumer goods, it took a civil war to end it.

We should not be shocked with skyrocketing STIs or marital and family breakdown. Nor when men rape women and children or even when children rape one another. These developments are entirely consistent with the explosive growth in pornography.

It's not harmless adult entertainment, as some would like us to believe, but a real, measurable and undeniable threat to individuals, families and society. The crucial question before us is not whether or not the state has a compelling interest in protecting society from the harm of pornography, but rather, given the overwhelming evidence of harm, why it chooses to do so little?

*"Despite high levels of exposure to pornography in venues such as the Internet, few negative effects are observed."*

# Pornography Is Not Addictive and Does Not Lead to Violence Against Women

*Daniel Linz*

*Daniel Linz is a professor of communication and the law and society at the University of California, Santa Barbara. His work on pornography and its effects on human behavior has recently appeared in the National Academy of Sciences' "Youth, Pornography and the Internet." In the following viewpoint he argues that there is no scientific proof that pornography is addictive or that viewing pornography leads to violence against women and children. He challenges assumptions about the nature of sex addiction and urges psychology professionals and the public to be skeptical about blanket statements regarding the dangers of Internet pornography.*

As you read, consider the following questions:

1. According to the author, what four findings can be concluded from the psychological research that has been conducted on sex addiction?

Daniel Linz, "Response to Testimony Before the United States Senate," *Free Speech Coalition*, 2005. Reproduced by permission of the author.

2. According to Aviel Goodman, what are some criteria for diagnosing an addictive disorder?

3. What did William Fisher conclude about the relationship of violent crimes to the accessibility of Internet pornography?

It has come to my attention that the Senate Committee on Commerce, Science, and Transportation held a hearing on "The Science Behind Pornography Addiction" on November 18, 2004. My understanding is that the Committee has allowed a two-week response period. I would like to take this opportunity to respond to the testimony of the several witnesses who testified before the committee. It is my opinion that a one-sided view of the "science" behind the notion of pornography exposure as addictive has been presented to the Committee. I would like to take the opportunity to present what I feel is a more objective overview of the state of scientific research than that expressed by the witnesses who appeared before the Committee.

Dr. [Judith] Reisman [president of the Institute for Media Education and author of numerous studies on the social consequences of pornography] makes the claim that: "Thanks to the latest advances in neuroscience, we now know that pornographic visual images imprint and alter the brain, triggering an instant, involuntary, but lasting, biochemical memory trail, arguably, subverting the First Amendment by overriding the cognitive speech process. This is true of so-called 'soft-core' and 'hard-core' pornography. And once new neurochemical pathways are established they are difficult or impossible to delete." Later she asserts: "These media erotic fantasies become deeply embedded . . . addicting many of those exposed."

It is indeed a psychological fact that many powerful messages and ideas leave strong memory traces. This is in no way unique to pornographic images. Dr. Reisman fails to distinguish the nature of strong memory traces resulting from other experiences from pornography in her work. She appears to believe that once the viewer is exposed to enough pornography he or she loses the capacity to reason or make intelligent judgments about the messages being conveyed in pornographic material and that other memory traces from equally or more profound experiences are overwhelmed by exposure and subsequent "addiction" to pornography. There is no scientifically credible evidence for her ideas.

## Questions About Sex Addiction

In fact, the notions of "sexual addiction" generally, including "pornography addiction" as well as the recent concern with "on-line sex addiction" are highly questionable to most scientists. Four findings seem to emerge from an unbiased examination of the psychological literature on sex addiction: 1) So-called sexual addiction may be nothing more than learned behavior that can be unlearned; 2) labels such as "sex addict" may tell us more about society's prejudices and the therapist doing the labeling than the client; 3) most research on pornography use, for example, through venues such as the Internet, is methodologically flawed; and, 4) scientists who have undertaken scientifically rigorous studies of exposure to sex materials report that despite high levels of exposure to pornography in venues such as the Internet, few negative effects are observed.

An addiction is commonly described as an experience of powerlessness, an unmanagable drive, and a basic out-of-control sexual behavior. "Sexual addiction" may be nothing more than a learned sexual behavior expressed in violation of prevailing societal norms and expectations. In our society today it appears to be in vogue to attribute numerous popular behaviors to biological and psychological origins. It is an explanation of convenience for something threatening and unpopular. [Researchers Martin P.] Levine, [and Richard] Troiden (1988) in their article "The Myth of Sexual Compulsivity" say that sex is not an addiction; it is an experience rather than a substance. "By definition, sex is not a state of physiological dependence and it does not lead to distress upon abrupt withdrawal," say Levine et al.

In the official bulletin for the American Psychological Association, *Monitor on Psychology*, volume 31, no. 4, April 2000, Tori DeAngelis reports that many other psychologists doubt that "addiction" is the right term to describe what happens to people when they spend too much time with sex materials on the Internet. "It seems misleading to characterize behaviors as 'addictions' on the basis that people say they do too much of them," says Sara Kiesler, PhD, a researcher at Carnegie Mellon University and co-author of one of the only controlled studies on Internet usage, published in the September 1998 *American Psychologist*. No research has yet established that there is a disorder of Internet sex addiction that is separable from problems such as loneliness or problem gambling, or that a passion for using the Internet is long-lasting. . . .

## Violence Against Women

If we know anything about pornography exposure and antisocial behaviors such as violence against women we know two things: 1) for the average person the message of violence as pleasurable to the woman must be present for negative effects to occur; and 2) for other forms of pornography the effects are an interaction between personality characteristics and exposure.

For example, [*The Question of Pornography Research Findings and Policy Implications* authors Daniel] Linz, [Edward] Donnerstein and [Steven] Penrod in a study reported in the *Journal of Personality and Social Psychology*, 1988, found that exposure to violent films depicting violence against women desensitized men who viewed them and rendered the men less sympathetic towards a victim of sexual assault they were later asked to evaluate for injuries. This same effect was not observed for nonviolent pornography.

Once we move from the laboratory to investigations involving men who report viewing pornography, the effects of sexually explicit materials are almost certainly a joint function of the personality characteristics of the individual who seeks out such materials and of exposure to such materials per se. . . .

## An Unofficial Label

Dr. [Mary Anne] Layden [co-director of the Sexual Trauma and Psychopathology program at the University of Pennsylvania's Center for Cognitive Therapy] puts forth the notion that: "For the viewer, pornography increases the likelihood of sexual addiction and they respond in ways similar to other addicts. Sexual addicts develop tolerance and will need more and harder kinds of pornographic material. They have escalating compulsive sexual behavior becoming more out of control and also experience withdrawal symptoms if they stop the use of the sexual material."

In fact, contrary to Dr. Layden's speculations the psychological and psychiatric community does not recognize "sexual addiction" and the related notion of "pornography addiction" as a distinct psychological disorder. The descriptive terms "sexual addiction" and "pornography addiction" do not appear in the current *Diagnostic and Statistical Manual of Mental Disorders (DSM-IV)*. According to Richard Irons, MD and Jennifer P. Schneider, MD, PhD, addiction professionals who encounter both compulsive and impulsive sexual acting-out behaviors in their patients have experienced too many conceptual and communication difficulties with mental health professionals and managed care organizations who utilize *DSM* terminology and diagnostic criteria. This difficulty in communication has fueled so much skepticism among psychiatrists and other mental health professionals regarding the

## The Myth of Sex Addiction

The diagnosis of "sex addiction" has become popular with both lay people and professionals in recent years. But it is a destructive and irresponsible one that should be discontinued. In 21 years as a marriage counselor and sex therapist, I've never seen a single case in which the label "sex addiction" was clinically useful. That's because there is no such thing. What we clinicians do frequently see includes:

- Poor decision-making: Even the healthiest people occasionally behave sexually in ways which later they regret.

- Poor impulse control: This, too, we all experience to one degree or another with money, food, TV, gossip, etc. Most of the time it is simply inconvenient; sometimes it gets out of hand.

- Obsessive-compulsive behavior: A small number of people think, feel, and do things that they don't want to do. Whether it's exhibitionism or hand washing, they are driven: the more they try to stop, the worse they feel, and the more they have to do it.

- Psychotic or sociopathic personalities: This small group of people has impaired reality—testing, and typically behaves with complete disregard for even the most basic social conventions.

*Marty Klein, "The Myth of Sex Addiction,"*
Sexual Intelligence: An Electronic Newsletter, *no. 1,*
*March 2000.*

case for including sex addiction as a mental disorder that they have not recognized such a classification. . . .

Based on his observations with compulsive sexual behavior as well as on the similarities between pathological gambling and addictive use of a substance, [psychologist Aviel] Goodman (1990) suggested a list of criteria for an addictive disorder. This list includes a recurrent failure to resist impulses to engage in a specified behavior; increasing sense of tension immediately prior to initiating the behavior; frequent engaging in the behavior when expected to fulfill occupational, academic, domestic or social obligations; and important social, occupational, or recreational activities given up or reduced because of the behavior. We have no evidence from psychological studies of pornography that any of this occurs. . . .

But, here is the rub. According to Goodman any behavior that is used to produce gratification and to escape internal discomfort can be engaged in compulsively and can constitute an addictive disorder. This would presumably mean that those who engage in obsessive Saturday afternoon college football viewing, Sunday afternoon professional football exposure, playing computer games, playing basketball to work up endorphins, as well as obsessive workaholics are all experiencing addictive disorders by this definition.

Finally, there is a real-life observation that is difficult to dispute. As an admittedly crude estimate of consequences of exposure to sexually explicit Internet materials on individuals who seek contact with such content, Dr. William Fisher in an article entitled "Internet Pornography: A Social Psychological Perspective on Internet Sexuality" in the *Journal of Sex Research* (2001) made an informative observation. He plotted rates of reported forcible rape in the United States from 1995 to 1999. This time interval is by all accounts a period of exponential growth in the availability and use of all forms of Internet sexually explicit materials. Although open to a variety of interpretations, he noted that the rate of reported forcible rape in the U.S. fell consistently and significantly throughout this time period of spectacular increase in access to and use of Internet sexually explicit materials of all kinds.

In summary, before rushing to the judgment that pornography is addicting, we must take note of the following: So-called sexual addiction may be nothing more than learned behavior that can be unlearned; labels such as "sex addict" may tell us more about society's prejudices and the therapist doing the labeling than the client; scientists who have undertaken scientifically rigorous studies of exposure to sex materials report that despite high levels of exposure to pornography in venues such as the Internet, few negative effects are observed. For the average person the message of violence against women must be present for negative effects to occur. For other forms of pornography, the effects are an interaction between personality and exposure to pornography. Professionals who encounter both compulsive and impulsive sexual acting-out behaviors in their patients have experienced too many conceptual problems with the notion of sex addiction to be able to separate their preconceived ideas from whatever pathology they may observe in their patients. This difficulty in communication has fueled so much skepticism among psychiatrists and other mental health professionals regarding the case for including sex addiction as a mental disorder that they have not recognized such a classification.

> *"Alcoholics Anonymous [AA] meetings and the AA way of life have been very therapeutic for me."*

# Alcoholics Anonymous Can Save a Marriage

### Michigan Dental Association (MDA)

*The Michigan Dental Association (MDA) is a professional orga- nization for dentists and dental associates throughout the state of Michigan. In the following viewpoint an MDA member tells his story about becoming an alcoholic and seeking help through Alcoholics Anonymous (AA). He argues that without AA he might never have been able to quit abusing alcohol and mari- juana. Through the program, he learned to appreciate his mar- riage, his family, and his life in general.*

As you read, consider the following questions:

1. How long did the author abuse drugs and alcohol be- fore seeking help?
2. For how many days in a row did the therapist recom- mend that the author attend AA meetings?
3. When do most AA meetings start?

So what was the big deal if I had a few beers after work?

I deserved it. Dentistry is an intense, challenging occupation. It felt good to drink three or four ice cold beers; it felt real good. Beer was like a magic elixir. It gave me a euphoric feeling and washed away the burdens and stresses of my day. It made me forget about the squabbling between my receptionist and hygienist, the slightly open contact on the posterior composite, or the over-filled root canal.

Alcohol was also a reward for some of the good dentistry I did. The crown prep on tooth number 15 that I did on the person with the nasty gag reflex, or the six maxillary veneers I placed that looked magnificent. Dentistry is a rewarding job, yet stressful. Alcohol just seemed to fit at the end of the day. I had a work-hard, play-hard attitude; I've come to discover many alcoholics have that similar trait.

Once that last patient was out of the chair, it was time for me to "play hard," and so every night a few beers and a little marijuana would send me off on an instant vacation. Since my back was often a little sore, I could also justify taking a Vicodin at the end of the day. The combination of beer, marijuana, and Vicodin made all the pain go away in a hurry.

I was feeling no pain, physically or mentally. Of course, I wouldn't go straight home. I went to golf league in the summer, or bowling in the winter. I would go to dental society meetings, or maybe just meet my buddies at the local pub for a little male bonding. All of these activities were reasons to continue drinking.

This was my lifestyle for over 20 years, and I saw no problems with it. I was doing some quality dentistry. My practice was growing. I was respected by my peers. My bills were paid. I'd never been arrested for drunk driving, or public intoxication. I exercised daily. My health was excellent. My life was great—or so I thought.

## Struggling Marriage

I'm also married, with three young children. But not surprisingly, my wife had become disenchanted with my lifestyle. I'd come home at whatever hour, slurring my words, smelling of booze and marijuana. I certainly wasn't interested in discussing any of the events of her day or mine. I just wanted to eat, watch TV, and fall asleep. I snored like a chainsaw. I was *not* someone you wanted to be married to. But, I felt my wife had nothing to complain about. In my very superficial, materialistic view of life, I thought we were living the perfect life. After all, we lived in a big house in a pleasant neighborhood. We had new cars, took numerous vacations. We were members of the country club, had a maid, even a lawn service. No, I thought our lives were enviable.

Well, my wife certainly didn't think so. The truth was, our marriage was going downhill fast. She was embarrassed and resentful of my drinking. I couldn't be trusted with our children. She was scared to death of the possibility of me driving with the kids in the car. She recognized the fact that I'd rather be drunk or high than be a functional husband and father.

After a hard night of drinking I'd wake up in the morning and with a vicious hangover—and I didn't sleep very well due to my alcohol-induced sleep apnea. I'd go to work in the morning smelling like a brewery. I was probably still legally drunk, and probably I was in no shape to do dentistry on anyone.

## Compulsive Drinking

My substance abuse problem was ruining my health, destroying my marriage, and endangering my patients' dental health. Although I was never arrested for drunk driving, I can't imagine how many hundreds of times I drove drunk, threatening my own life and everyone else on the road. And yet even with all these problems, I somehow remained oblivious to them. I didn't want to stop drinking, not at all. Drinking to me was

153

synonymous with having fun. Parties were more fun. Golfing, skiing, going to sporting events, and so on were just that much more enjoyable if I was drinking, and I certainly didn't want to stop having fun. Therefore, I had no plans to stop drinking. But more importantly, I *couldn't* stop. Twenty-some years of drinking and drugging made me physically and psychologically dependent on alcohol and drugs.

I had become an addict. It took more and more alcohol to obtain the effect that I was looking for. I didn't admit that I was an alcoholic, because I wasn't a stereotypical skid row bum. I was a well-educated, upper-middle-class dentist, a functioning human being in good health. But you see, alcoholism is a cunning baffling disease, and its most insidious symptom is the alcoholic's denial that they even have the disease. This denial is even more prevalent amongst us health professionals. We're used to being the healers; we aren't used to being the ones that need to be healed.

Frankly, I was obsessed with my drinking. I planned my day around when I could start drinking. I hated being sober. I'd gone from enjoying a few beers after work to *needing* a few beers after work. I needed to drink to make my life tolerable. Many times I wished I wasn't a dentist. I dreamed of being in an occupation such as a musician, a playwright, or a journalist. That way I could justify using mind-altering substances all day long, because it would enhance my creativity, or so I thought. Beer and marijuana were my best friends. Nothing else really mattered to me except catching a buzz.

After tolerating me for nearly 16 years, my wife had had enough of my self-indulgent behavior. She became quite upset, began seeing a psychotherapist, and eventually asked me to leave. She said that if I don't sober up, that she wanted a divorce. That scared me. I didn't know where to turn or what to do. I didn't want to lose my wife, my family, or my perception of a perfect life.

# Seeking Help

I went to my wife's psychotherapist, pleading for her help to some way save my marriage. The psychotherapist told me something very interesting. She said, "Don't worry about saving your marriage. You first have to save yourself." No, she didn't mince words. She pulled within 10 inches of my face and said to me, directly: "You are an alcoholic, and alcohol is screwing up what could be a wonderful life for you."

She emphasized how difficult recovery would be: How I would have to recover for myself and not to save my marriage or for my wife or for my children. She suggested that I go to a treatment center, and she suggested that I start going to Alcoholics Anonymous [AA] meetings. Well, the treatment center involved leaving my practice for a month, and I wondered how I would be able to explain to my patients or to my employees where I was and why I went away for a month. Plus, I'd lose a month's worth of income and perhaps quite a few patients. I didn't go to the treatment center, but I did agree to start going to Alcoholics Anonymous meetings. The therapist said I needed to go to 90 meetings in 90 days, and then continue to go to AA meetings on a regular basis for the rest of my life. She said that my alcoholism is a permanent disease and I would never completely recover, but would only keep it in remission. I was willing to do anything to help save my marriage, so I agreed. But I couldn't understand how AA meetings were going to help. How would listening to a bunch of grizzly old men in a church basement help me stop drinking?

Well, two days after my session with the psychotherapist, I went to an AA meeting. It wasn't what I expected. These people weren't wretched drunks or grizzly old men. I found a pleasant mix of approximately 30 people, men and women from the ages of 19 to their mid-60s. They were well groomed, they were upbeat, and they all seemed happy to be there. Each

# What Is Alcoholics Anonymous?

Following is the definition of A.A. [Alcoholics Anonymous] appearing in the Fellowship's basic literature and cited frequently at meetings of A.A. groups:

> Alcoholics Anonymous is a fellowship of men and women who share their experience, strength and hope with each other that they may solve their common problem and help others to recover from alcoholism.

> The only requirement for membership is a desire to stop drinking. There are no dues or fees for A.A. membership; we are self-supporting through our own contributions. A.A. is not allied with any sect, denomination, politics, organization or institution; does not wish to engage in any controversy; neither endorses nor opposes any causes. Our primary purpose is to stay sober and help other alcoholics to achieve sobriety.

> Alcoholics Anonymous can also be defined as an informal society of more than 2,000,000 recovered alcoholics in the United States, Canada, and other countries. These man and women meet in local groups, which range in size from a handful in some localities to many hundreds in larger communities.

> Currently, women make up 35 percent of the total membership.

*Alcoholics Anonymous,*
*"What Is Alcoholics Anonymous?" 2008.*
*www.alcoholics-anonymous.org.*

of them spoke about how much better their lives had become since surrendering to their alcoholism. They seemed content.

It was explained to me during that first meeting night that I didn't need to stop drinking for the rest of my life. I just needed to stop drinking for the next 24 hours, and then go to another meeting tomorrow night. They also said that stopping drinking wasn't going to change the world, but that it would change my perception of the world. My recovery would be hard; it is very hard to quit drinking. I had to make it my highest priority. Sobriety had to be the most important thing in my life.

I went to a meeting the next night. Most AA meetings start at 8 p.m. This is a strategic time, because alcoholics usually start drinking well before 8 o'clock and it's pretty embarrassing to go to an AA meeting when you're drunk. So, in the early days of my recovery I had to "white-knuckle" it through those two to three hours between finishing my last patient and finally going to that night's meeting.

## Life Lessons

Those first few weeks and months were very hard. Drinking was a way of life for me. It was nearly 60 days of going to at least one, if not sometimes two meetings a day before I noticed a slight decrease in my desire to drink. About this same time, I also realized I LIKE going to meetings. I always felt better after a meeting. I began to understand the benefits of group therapy, the concept of sharing my failures and successes of each day and then listening to others share their experiences. It gave me an appreciation of my life, and sense of gratitude that I'd never felt before. I developed a respect and admiration for my fellow recovering alcoholics, as many of them had been through a lot more troubles than I had ever imagined. Yet, many were very much like me. Some didn't necessarily hit rock bottom; they were never in jail, they were never mentally or physically seriously ill, and in fact most of them were quite intelligent. They were college professors, attorneys, businessmen, soccer moms, nurses, physicians, musicians, journalists, and other dentists. These people were from all walks of life, from all socio-economic strata, from Yale to jail, from Park Avenue to park benches. But the one thing we all had in common was that we all recognized the detrimental effect that alcohol and substance abuse had on our lives.

What an education I got from the people who were from dysfunctional families—how many of them were brought up by alcoholics, and how alcoholism and drug abuse affected their entire family. Alcoholism is genetically and environmentally passed from one generation to the next. This legacy of alcoholism is very difficult for many people to overcome. It made me realize how lucky I was that I had come from a loving family, that I had the opportunity to go to college and dental school. It made me appreciate the fact that my parents were not alcoholic and that they loved me very much. It also made me realize that I will do everything I can to make sure that my children do not become alcoholics.

Alcoholics Anonymous meetings and the AA way of life have been very therapeutic for me. AA has changed me in many ways. It's not just about not drinking. It's taught me the coping skills I need to live comfortably in an often uncomfortable world. AA has helped me comprehend how much I love my life, how much I love my children and my wife. I've grown to appreciate what a privilege it is to be a dentist. Dentistry continues to be a challenging profession, and life can still be difficult, but I've learned to be humble. I'm only human, and I make mistakes, but instead of hiding from them in a beer bottle, I now face these mistakes head-on. I learn from them, and do everything I can to correct my mistakes.

I've also learned that I don't need to drink to have fun. The friends I've made in Alcoholics Anonymous can have an awful lot of fun without drinking. I have also discovered that many of my old "drinking buddies" really didn't drink as much as I thought they did. They would stop after one or two beers, or they didn't drink at all. They didn't get drunk at every opportunity like I did.

I have also learned what a great feeling it is to wake up in the morning without a hangover. It's been said that no one ever has woken up in the morning wishing he had gotten drunk the night before. . . .

Recovery is very hard. It was hard for me; it's hard for most people. If you're an alcoholic or an addict, you need all the help you can get. It's nice just to talk with someone who has experienced the same problems you have. A problem shared is a problem cut in half.

I've gained a lot of spirituality going to Alcoholics Anonymous, and I don't mean that I've become a better Catholic or more religious. I mean that I have come to realize how precious life is, and that I don't want to waste it. If you are experiencing any financial, marital, legal, emotional, social, health or spiritual problems in your life, and you think that drugs or alcohol are contributing to these problems, then seek help. Call someone. Give it a try. Sometimes having a few beers after work may not be as innocent as it originally appears. As in my case, it may lead to a life that spirals out of control.

*"I have learned to see AA [Alcoholics
Anonymous] as a sort of infuriating,
doting mother-in-law."*

# Alcoholics Anonymous Can Challenge a Marriage

*Mary Barrett*

*In the following viewpoint Mary Barrett, a regular contributor
to the* Daily Mail, *writes about dealing with her alcoholic
husband's recovery. Contrary to most accounts, she struggled
with her husband's journey through Alcoholics Anonymous. In
addition, she felt excluded from his treatment since she was
rarely welcome at his regular meetings and did not find Al-Anon
meetings, set up for friends and family members of alcoholics,
helpful. Although she is grateful that her husband is no longer
abusing alcohol, she wishes that the difficulties spouses face while
their partners are in recovery were more frequently brought to
light.*

As you read, consider the following questions:

1. How did the author's husband spend every evening of
   his first three months of sobriety?

Mary Barrett, "Sobriety Made My Husband a Stranger," *Mail Online*, October 22, 2006,
pp. 1–5. Copyright © 2006 Associated Newspapers Limited. Reproduced by permission.

2. Why does the author accompany her husband to an AA meeting once a year?

3. How does the author's husband handle his wife's drinking?

I'll never forget the summer's evening nine years ago, when the man came to take my husband away.

My husband, John, is a big man, with a deep, rumbling voice, and a commanding, and usually cheerful, presence. He was neither cheerful nor commanding that evening.

He answered the door, greeted the man without introducing me, and followed submissively into the waiting car. Alcoholics Anonymous [AA] had entered my life.

The man was John's sponsor. Now I can see that it was the best thing that could have happened to us. But then, all I could feel was anger, confusion, hurt, and, above all, deep, deep fear.

John and I had been married for just over two years at the time, and, believe it or not, I had not even seen this coming. Oh, I knew we had problems.

We are both strong and stubborn personalities, and were both entering our first marriages at the age of around forty, having been together for a year; there was a lot of love between us, but there were an awful lot of fights, too.

No big deal, I told myself, just part of the process of learning to live with someone.

There was stress, as well. He works in computers at a nose bleedingly high level involving long hours and high pressure, and besides we were going through the emotional hell of trying (unsuccessfully, alas) for a late life baby.

We both liked to drink, and if lately he had started to drink a little more than usual—well, he wasn't the one who was either trying to get pregnant or having miscarriages, so why not?

Besides, he had recently developed diabetes, and the doctor had told him to cut down, which he said he was doing. So everything was under control. Right?

One bank holiday Monday, I arrived home to find him slumped and dazed in front of his computer.

There was a glass of clear liquid beside him which he swore was water, and I had no way of knowing otherwise, since (strange, but true) I was born without a sense of smell.

## Frightening

If not drunk, he was undergoing a dangerous diabetes sugar low, whose symptoms are alarmingly similar.

I made him a peanut butter sandwich. He threw it into my face and stormed out of the house. It was the worst fight we had had, and certainly the most frightening.

The next day, he returned from work later than usual and bearing a bombshell. He was an alcoholic, he said.

He was not just someone who liked to relax with a drink in the evenings, but someone who, had been stopping off to buy his own secret stash of drink on the way home, consuming it in the car, and arriving home half-cut—although until then, he had been hiding it well—to begin drinking all over again from the extremely well-stocked drinks cabinet we kept in the house. That was all about to change, he said.

He had indeed been terribly drunk last night, he said, and had woken that morning with not only a throbbing head but also a strong sense of what he must do next.

He had that very evening attended his first Alcoholics Anonymous meeting, he told me. He had found a sponsor there, who would pick him up the next night to go to another meeting.

## Addiction

He would take the rest of his life one day at a time, he said, slipping already into the language of recovering addiction which over the years would become so familiar.

But his resolution was that he would never drink again.

I was gobsmacked to put it mildly. I'd been expecting an apology for my ruined evening, hoping for a bunch of flowers.

Instead, I learned that for a considerable period of time my husband had been deceiving me with a frankly disturbing degree of conviction.

That for the great majority of our three-year relationship, he had been more or less drunk (Had he been drunk when he first told me he loved me? Drunk when he proposed?).

That today, without consulting me, he had decided to give up all the lovely bottles of wine and sparkling cocktails that we enjoyed sharing, and throw in his lot with a bunch of complete strangers who sat on hard chairs in church halls.

How did I feel? Well—how would YOU feel?

Alcoholics Anonymous guidelines advise that in the first ninety days of sobriety, the member should attend ninety meetings.

So during the first three months of his new life, John spent every weekday evening and weekend morning at an AA meeting.

## Loneliness

Those hours cemented his commitment to sobriety, I understand that. But I can't remember that time without feeling my heart sink into a hole of loneliness and fear.

There was no one—no one—I could turn to for support.

I have no immediate family left, and my friends, while sympathetic, knew even less about alcoholism than I did.

And John—who was, after all, facing a major and traumatic life change—had scant time for my worries.

But they were there, all right, and I had three months of long, lonely evenings to face them. How could he have lied to me so efficiently and for so long?

If he had been drunk until now, would he still love me when sober? Who were these people he spent all his time with instead of me, who confided to him secrets that he was not allowed to share with his wife?

I knew next to nothing about AA, and its members do not welcome "normies" (as they charmingly refer to non-alcoholics) to its meetings. When I tried to ask John to explain, the only response I got was a terse, "Go to Al Anon."

Al Anon is the organization for the families of addicts, and to anyone who is going through the heartbreak of watching a loved one self-destruct, I would unhesitatingly recommend it.

I have also met other people whose addicted family member, like mine, has been sober for years, who have found great support there.

While it works for a lot of people, it just didn't do it for me.

I never actually had to deal with John's active alcoholism, because the first I consciously learned of it was when he told me he was addressing it.

So I didn't need to be told how to detach from my loved one's drunken behaviour because, by the time I went there, he was no longer drunk.

## Selfish

What I did need, and quite badly, was to be encouraged that the changes that he was going through would prove to be for the best in the end; to be counseled on how to get over the fact that my husband had looked me in the face and lied to me throughout our marriage; to be reassured that, no, it is not monstrously selfish, but only human, for me to mourn the fact that he and I will never toast each other in fine wine again.

This was something I had to work out painfully and alone.

## What Is Alcoholism?

Alcoholism, also known as "alcohol dependence," is a disease that includes four symptoms:

### Craving:

A strong need, or compulsion, to drink.

### Loss of control:

The inability to limit one's drinking on any given occasion.

### Physical dependence:

Withdrawal symptoms, such as nausea, sweating, shakiness, and anxiety, occur when alcohol use is stopped after a period of heavy drinking.

### Tolerance:

The need to drink greater amounts of alcohol in order to "get high."

*National Institute on Alcohol Abuse and Alcoholism,*
*"Alcoholism Getting the Facts: NIAA,"*
*November 13, 2001. www.wrongdiagnosis.com.*

Gradually I did so, and of course life is far better with him sober than it ever was with him drunk.

We hardly ever fight these days, and his health has improved immeasurably—he has returned to the charming, exuberant, and affectionate man I married, with the only difference being that the liquid in his glass is a different colour and he no longer falls asleep at the end of dinner parties.

I admire him more than I can say for having been wise enough to identify his own problem and brave enough to tackle it; he says—now!—that he is grateful that I stuck with him through the bad times.

But inevitably, sobriety means changes, and one is that Alcoholics Anonymous has now become part of our lives.

John attends a meeting every Sunday morning, and I accompany him once a year on his "sobriety birthday"—the anniversary of the day he gave up drinking—to present him with a cake.

They're a clannish bunch, are recovering alcoholics, and when they crowd around John with backslaps and congratulations on another year accomplished, it never seems to occur to them that I am also in his life, helping him, supporting him, seeking out exotic soft drinks to replace the wine. But I'm used to that now.

I used to rage, but over the years, I have learned to see AA as a sort of infuriating, doting mother-in-law—tactless and altogether without consideration for me, but she isn't going to go away, and let's face it, without her, John would not be here.

## Tolerant

I am lucky to be able to enjoy alcohol without being addicted to it, and lucky, too, that John, unlike many recovering alcoholics, is extremely tolerant about other people's drinking—he says he actively wants other people to be able to behave normally around him.

He only requests that I keep strong liquor a smell's distance from him, and that he not be asked to go out and buy it.

(The bad news is that I now have to do all the shopping when we give a party; the good, that at the end, he is still awake enough to help clear up).

He's perfectly happy to talk about his recovery, too, and among our social circle has become something of an unofficial authority, someone our friends will go to when they have questions—What's it like never to drink? What's it like to be an alcoholic? Is my partner/colleague/friend one? . . . Am I one? . . .

Inevitably, we've lost some friendships—the old school pal of his who just stopped answering the telephone, apparently afraid that sobriety might be catching; the about-to-be-former girlfriend of mine who kept warning me that "if you don't quit, too, he'll start again, and it will be your fault"—but the ones we have kept, like our marriage, have grown deeper.

I've told John that if he ever falls off the wagon, we will deal with it together; but that if he ever lies to me again, we will be in real trouble.

I am still not quite sure if he knows just how badly he hurt me by lying all those years ago; what he says now—in the snappy language of twelve-step catch-phrases in which he is now fluent—is that he had been "lying to himself as much as to me," that alcohol is "cunning, baffling, and powerful," and that we were both lucky that he came to his senses before he ended up "in prison, in hospital, or dead."

(I shouldn't make fun of the clichés—they irritate me, but help him in his struggle, which is far more important).

I have forgiven him the lies, as he has forgiven me for many things over the years; I am only grateful that he was able to stop both the lying and the drink, before real damage was done.

He has not fallen off the wagon, by the way, and oddly enough, it's not something I worry about.

As he was able to drink without my help, I trust that he will stay sober without it, too.

I sometimes miss splitting a bottle of wine with him; I sometimes am sad to think that we will never again break out a celebratory bottle of champagne.

But he is here, and he is healthy, and we are, if anything, more deeply in love than ever.

Now, if only Alcoholics Anonymous would give out a birthday cake to spouses. . . .

# Periodical Bibliography

*The following articles have been selected to supplement the diverse views presented in this chapter.*

Dale Burke — "The Bane of Ritalin Addiction," *Hinduism Today*, October–December 2008.

Oriella Cattapan and Jolyon Grimwade — "Parental Illicit Drug Use and Family Life: Reports from Those Who Sought Help," *Australian and New Zealand Journal of Family Therapy*, June 2008.

Melissa Daly — "Meth: Isn't Worth Messing With," *Current Health 2*, September 2008.

Gail Echeverria — "A Mother's Cry: A Professional's Experience Doesn't Diminish the Pain of Family Addiction, or the Questions," *Addiction Professional*, September–October 2006.

Elspeth Loades — "Drug Addiction and Families," *Community Care*, July 5, 2007.

Pamela Paul — "The Porn Factor," *Time*, January 19, 2004.

Vicki Sheff-Cahan — "A Daughter's Secret," *People*, January 29, 2007.

Douglas C. Smith and James A. Hall — "Strengths-Oriented Family Therapy for Adolescents with Substance Abuse Problems," *Social Work*, vol. 53, no. 2, April 2008.

Alexandra Stanbury and Mark Griffiths — "Is Obsessive Love an Addiction?" *Psychology Review*, February 2007.

John Throop — "Cyber-Addictions," *Marriage Partnership*, Summer 2007.

Stephen W. Tracy, John F. Kelly, and Rudolf H. Moos — "The Influence of Partner Status, Relationship Quality and Relationship Stability on Outcomes Following Intensive Substance-Use Disorder Treatment," *Journal of Studies on Alcohol*, July 2005.

# CHAPTER 4

# How Can Addictions Be Treated?

# Chapter Preface

There seems to be as many addiction treatment methods as there are types of addictions, and no one approach will cure all addicts. Although treatment can be expensive, the benefits to society and self make it worth the cost. Estimates made by the National Institute on Drug Abuse (NIDA) state that "every $1 invested in addiction treatment programs yields a return of between $4 and $7 in reduced drug-related crime, criminal justice costs, and theft alone." Despite these potential gains, some people have begun to question whether it is appropriate for judges to sentence offenders to mandatory drug rehabilitation.

In criminal cases where the defendant is found to be abusing drugs or alcohol, some judges sentence the offenders to drug rehabilitation programs as an alternative to incarceration. Recovering addicts who have found success in court-ordered drug rehabilitation insist that it saved their lives. Ken Jackson (pseudonym) states that he never would have attempted to quit drugs and alcohol if not for a judge who ordered him to attend Alcoholics Anonymous (AA) meetings or spend three years in jail for felony drug possession. His nearly twenty years of sobriety "are due largely to that moment in the courtroom." Many judges and states across the country began to embrace this approach in the 1980s in an effort not only to help addicts overcome their addictions but to reduce the prison population as well.

However, critics of mandatory drug rehabilitation sentencing argue that given that the majority of drug programs are founded on or are heavily influenced by 12-step programs, like Alcoholics Anonymous, the courts are trying to push religious-based treatment in a secular justice system. The National Treatment Center Study found that 93 percent of private treatment programs and nearly 100 percent of publicly funded treatment programs are founded on the 12-step approach, which requires a belief in a higher power (not necessarily the Christian God). In fact, in 1999 the Supreme Court ruled that sentencing criminals to AA meetings is unconstitutional due to the "deeply religious nature" of the organization. The ruling was upheld in 2007 in the Ninth U.S. Circuit Court of Appeals in San Francisco, which stated that "requiring a parolee to attend religion-based treatment programs violates the First Amendment."

The results of these rulings have put some judges at a loss for ways of helping addicts gain sobriety, and therefore, potentially lower the rates of re-offending. Nonetheless, questions about the justice system's role in helping addicts will continue, especially given that no one treatment works for all people. The authors in this chapter explore a variety of those treatment options with the goal of determining the best possible means of aiding addicts in overcoming their addictions.

*"The heroin injection pilots are well worth pursuing, both for the individual patient and for society as a whole."*

# Drug Clinics Are Effective at Treating Heroin Addiction

**Barry Nelson**

*In the following viewpoint Barry Nelson, a United Kingdom-based writer, argues that drug clinics may provide an answer to heroin addiction. He describes recent efforts by the United Kingdom's National Health Services to test the effectiveness of clinics that offer government-funded heroin injections twice daily to addicts in exchange for enrollment in a treatment program. Using testimony from two addicts enrolled in the program, Nelson asserts that the costs of operating these clinics are worth the long-term societal benefits.*

As you read, consider the following questions:

1. What slang phrase is used to refer to the heroin clinics set up in the United Kingdom?
2. Where did the heroin clinics originate?
3. How much more likely are heroin addicts who are not in treatment programs to die?

It is sobering to think that even in a relatively small town like Darlington, [England,] there is no shortage of hardened heroin addicts to enroll on a pioneering new treatment regime. The scale of heroin addiction in the UK these days means that, two years since it was established [in 2006], 33 people have voluntarily joined the project.

## A Simple Plan

The aim is simple. Offer safe, clean, injectable heroin to addicts twice a day in exchange for full cooperation with treatment. The idea behind what have become known as "shooting galleries" is to try to bring into structured environment a minority of heroin users who have not responded to more conventional treatment.

For the last two years [2006–2008], selected heroin addicts in Darlington have been able to get twice-daily injections of pure heroin at an NHS [National Health Services] clinic which costs £350,000 a year to run.

The scheme is aimed at addicts who have not responded to a methodone maintenance programme and was set up to see whether providing injectable heroin could bring a hardcore of chaotic drug users into regular NHS treatment.

Whatever our views of such treatment centres, heroin-abusers in Darlington are relatively lucky—the town's clinic is one of only three in the whole of England.

## Better than Methadone

In the UK most established heroin addicts are signed up to treatment programmes which give them daily doses of heroin-substitute, a linctus containing methadone which is taken orally. The theory behind this approach is that it is better for the addict and for society if their craving for drugs is met by the NHS rather than by breaking into cars or shoplifting to get the money to feed their habit.

For many heroin users, this approach works and they are able to lead a more normal life while efforts are made to wean them off drugs altogether.

So far, so good. But what if the hold that heroin has on some individuals is so great that they take the methadone handed out at their local clinic and carry on thieving to buy the street heroin they crave?

It was the Swiss who first came up with the idea of trying to "tame" out-of-control heroin addicts by offering them injectable heroin in supervised facilities in exchange for them enrolling in treatment.

Dr. Tom Carnwath, clinical director of addiction services for Tees, Esk and Wear Valley NHS Trust, was impressed by the Swiss approach to problem heroin users and was keen to try it in the UK. He got his chance a couple of years ago when a joint Department of Health and Home Office pilot scheme authorised the setting up of "shooting galleries", initially in Darlington and London and, more recently, in Brighton.

## Early Successes

Dr. Carnwath has been impressed by the impact of the Darlington project, which has grown from 16 clients to 33. Efforts are now being made to recruit another 15 or 16 addicts.

He argues that maintaining a hardcore of addicts on injectable heroin curbs their chaotic lifestyle and allows health care workers to support them in coming off illicit drugs.

While the scheme is not cheap, experts argue it is offset by savings to the healthcare and criminal justice services.

There is also a welfare issue, as heroin addicts who are not in treatment are 18 times more likely to die prematurely. Many of the addicts enrolled on the Darlington scheme have dependent young families and being in treatment has stabilised them and allowed them to spend more time with their children.

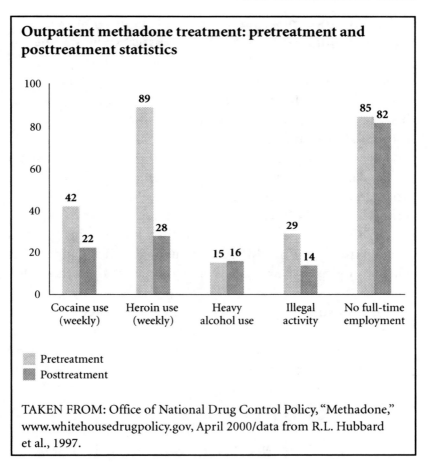

Outpatient methadone treatment: pretreatment and posttreatment statistics

TAKEN FROM: Office of National Drug Control Policy, "Methadone," www.whitehousedrugpolicy.gov, April 2000/data from R.L. Hubbard et al., 1997.

Last week [March 2008], Home Secretary Jacqui Smith announced a new ten-year strategy to meet the challenge of illegal drug use.

The Government says its previous strategy has reduced drug use to an 11-year low and drug-related crime by 20 per cent in the last five years.

On the treatment side, the Government wants to see the three heroin pilot schemes continue although it is not clear whether they are likely to be rolled out to the rest of the country.

That is good news for heroin addicts like Jon, 29, from Darlington, who has battled his addiction since he was a teenager.

Jon, which is not his real name, is blunt about the impact of the clinic. "By now, I would have been dead if it wasn't for this trial—either that or my legs would have been amputated in hospital," he says.

Jon was on street heroin for 12 years. He was so desperate for his daily fix that he was reduced to injecting himself in his groin or even in open wounds. "If they stopped this now, I reckon I would be back in jail or hospital," he says.

Dr. Carnwath is in no doubt that the heroin clinic is worthwhile. "Getting difficult to manage addicts onto this scheme improves their chance of leading a more normal life," he says.

The consultant psychiatrist visited the sister project at Brighton last week and met doctors and nurses who set up the service on the south coast six months ago. "They have 30 people already, London has about 50 and we are aiming for about 48 or 49," says Dr. Carnwath.

## Debunking Sceptics

In drug treatment circles the idea of giving addicts pure, injectable heroin on the NHS has been around for some time, but outside there has been some scepticism [skepticism]. Isn't the scheme simply turning the state into a drug pusher? And couldn't the money perhaps be better spent on expensive cancer drugs rejected by the National Institute for Health and Clinical Excellence on the grounds that they are not cost effective enough for the NHS?

But Dr. Carnwath is adamant that the heroin injection pilots are well worth pursuing, both for the individual patient and for society as a whole. "It is a means to an end."

"We have to try to get these people into treatment," he says.

The Government points to research which suggests that signing up addicts to treatment plans in exchange for methadone—and in the Darlington clinic's case, heroin—means that every pound spent in this way saves the State £9.50 in costs to the NHS or to the criminal justice system.

Dr. Carnwath says long-term methadone maintenance is a proven way to get people off drugs.

"The normal figure for methadone is ten per cent drug free in the first year and five per cent in subsequent years," he says. "After about ten years most are off the methadone.

"The trial here in Darlington and at the other two centres will show whether this approach is successful or not," Dr. Carnwath adds. "Certainly, the initial findings are quite hopeful."

Ian, another heroin addict signed up at the Darlington clinic, has the last word.

"All heroin addicts put their families through hell," he says. "You have to really want to sort yourself out to get on this trial.

"If they keep this going they will save money in the long run. How much does it cost to keep people in jail?"

> "To allow addicts with an addiction to opiates which are of a lower grade than Methadone on the program is completely insane."

# Drug Clinics Are Not Effective at Treating All Opiate Addictions

*Jean Sparks-Carreker*

*In the following viewpoint Jean Sparks-Carreker, a writer based in Birmingham, Alabama, recounts her experiences with pain pill addiction and her attempts at recovery through the use of a clinic that administered methadone. While she acknowledges that methadone clinics might be useful for patients addicted to heroin, she argues that this treatment method is dangerous for patients addicted to other opiates. Sparks-Carreker claims that she became addicted to the methadone and that her mental and physical condition became worse than before she underwent treatment.*

As you read, consider the following questions:

1. Why did the nurse make the author open her mouth after receiving her dose of methadone?

Jean Sparks-Carreker, "Methadone: The Cure for Opiate Addiction?" *American Chronicle*, April 11, 2007, pp. 1–3. Copyright © 2007 Ultio LLC. Reproduced by permission.

2. How much did the author pay for each dose of methadone?

3. What does "on the nod" mean?

According to the Office of National Drug Control Policy, "Methadone is a rigorously well-tested medication that is safe and efficacious for the treatment of narcotic withdrawal and dependence."

Years ago, I believed that I could not give up my little pain pill habit. Lortab, Lorcet, Tylox, whatever opioid pill I could con out of a doctor or buy for about $4 a pill on the streets, I usually took no more than eight in a twenty-four hour period, and had "weaned" down to about five a day when I decided I needed to get help. That was years ago, when I truly did not understand what a drug addiction could tragically become.

## Looking for Support

I started thumbing through the phone book in search of rehabilitative support. The group thing didn't appeal to me. I wanted relief from withdrawals, even though a small five pill a day habit was not, I had yet to learn, hard withdrawals from a drug. I found a Methadone Maintenance Program here in Jefferson County [Alabama] that promised relief from withdrawals while giving professional support and counseling to rid me of my addiction to hydrocodone. I was amazed.

The next day, I was up at dawn waiting to be seen by a doctor at the Methadone clinic. I noticed that even though the doors to the clinic were yet to be unlocked, there were about twenty to thirty people waiting outside. Once open for business, the nurse took down my information, and I was ushered through the process of a blood test, paying a $60 fee to begin the Methadone Maintenance Program, and finally was placed in a line in the main lobby, behind other Methadone patients.

When it came my turn at the Methadone clinic's dosing window, enclosed behind steel bars and offering a counter at

## Methadone Kills

Deaths from methadone are by no means negligible in number. In Florida in 2001, deaths from methadone poisoning surpassed those from heroin poisoning for the first time, by 133 to 121. Meanwhile, back in Blighty, [England] to demonstrate that we are also in the vanguard of modernity, deaths from methadone have been rising steadily. Between 1993 and 2000, there were 4,058 deaths from the direct effects of heroin; in the same period, there were 2,500 deaths from methadone. Since far fewer than a third of addicts receive methadone, it is at least as likely, to put it no stronger, that methadone kills rather than saves.

*Theodore Dalrymple, "An Official License Kill,"*
New Statesman, *March 3, 2003.*

my immediate front, I was told to sign my name. I paid her $11 to dose. The nurse, locked in a small room that held many, many rows of small plastic bottles containing Methadone on shelves that ran the length and height of the room, used a small knife to cut open the foil seal on the top of evidently my prescribed bottle. She then poured water into the bottle of Methadone, bringing the amount of liquid about 3/4 full. She handed this through the small window and placed it on the counter before me, instructing me to drink it all in front of her. I obeyed. The Methadone tasted horrible, even when diluted with water. She offered a small, paper cup of water and told me to drink that in front of her as well. I did. Then she wanted to see inside my mouth. At first, I was perplexed, then realized she wanted to make sure I did not leave with any Methadone in my mouth. They had prescribed me 30mgs [milligrams] of Methadone.

The few clues that should have warned me against Methadone Maintenance escaped me then, as I ignorantly believed that hydrocodone addiction was the worst addiction one could have. I should have looked at the fact that people will wait outside the clinic doors in freezing cold weather just to be able to be the first in line at the Methadone clinic's counter. I should have realized that if they are worried one may actually take the Methadone outside the clinic in their mouths, there must be someone willing to then buy the Methadone that had once been inside that patient's mouth. It did not occur to me, however, that my measly little pill addiction was not something that would cause that behavior. I would never have bought a pill someone smuggled to me inside their mouth. No way. It did not occur to me that perhaps Methadone was a drug that could cause someone to be that desperate in obtaining more.

## A Methadone High

That first day, however, nothing anyone could have told me would have ever swayed my support of this ingenious little answer known as Methadone Maintenance. I was on cloud nine, if there ever were such a place. Methadone was it, buddy, and if you didn't think so, you just had not tried it before. I was higher than I had ever been on any other opiate, and for that matter, on any other drug I had tried up until Methadone. It was the god of highs. It was my answer. And the very next morning, bright and early, I was up and standing in that line, ready to receive that second dose of 30mgs, which I actually did not need because I was still as high as a freaking kite. Upon standing once again at that counter and peering into the window at the seemingly imprisoned nurse, I went through the signing and paying routine, again only $11, and was then asked, "Is 30mgs holding you?" I answered that it was, and she told me that if it does not, I can go up 5 more milligrams. In fact, a Methadone Maintenance patient at that time could go up 5mgs a day until they reached 50mgs. At that point, they could increase another 10mgs a day until they reached 100mgs. And the $11 per day remained the same, no matter what milligram a Methadone Maintenance patient dosed at. These days, the milligram allowed is much higher per day.

I continued in this manner until I grew a tolerance for my little 30mgs of Methadone per day. It just wasn't "holding" me, I suppose. The fact was, it wasn't holding my high steadily until the next morning when I would again be able to dose. Over the next few months, I increased all the way to 100 mgs per day. I had no idea then that I had traded the hydrocodone monkey on my back for a completely insane gorilla. I eventually had to quit driving, being what a heroine addict would call "on the nod" continuously. It was like having Narcolepsy, where someone just falls asleep no matter what they are doing. I could not function as a normal adult. I could not function at all, and quite a few times, was escorted into the clinic by my husband and a friend, and held up so that I would not fall down in line, in order to dose for the day.

## Methadone Withdrawal

Withdrawing from Methadone was something I had never encountered before. No sickness, no flu, no pneumonia could even come close in comparison. It was like someone forcing their hand through my gut and pulling my spine from me. That is, before I broke with reality. After the break, I don't remember very much pain from the Methadone withdrawals. I only remember trying frantically to figure out who I was, who my loved ones were, and what was happening to me.

I had decided to come off Methadone, as it was destroying my life. I had not been told that coming off of it too quickly could cause severe problems. I was at about 80mgs per day when I decided to come down 5mgs per day and stop going to the Methadone clinic. When I reached about 40mgs, I have been told by my husband that I told the nurse I did not trust what they were giving me, and refused to dose. The doctor told my husband that I must be taking other drugs and lying about it, though my urinalysis were all clean. They told him they could do nothing for me.

My husband had to take off from work and sit with me twenty-four hours a day, as I would not sleep. I do not remember much from that time, but I do remember trying to throw myself from the truck when we were going down the Interstate one time. I don't know why. I didn't want to die. At least, I don't think I did.

Perhaps Methadone Maintenance Programs are beneficial to heroine addicts. I am not suggesting that no one benefits from the program at all. But to allow addicts with an addiction to opiates which are of a lower grade than Methadone on the program is completely insane, and even rings a familiarity to a common street dealer. As a matter of fact, I have often thought of Methadone clinics as the governments own legal drug deals. And Uncle Sam has one potent high awaiting anyone with any opiate addiction, even to Tylenol 3 with Codeine, right behind that little dosing counter. I have seen it, and thank God I lived through it. Many do not. Some even believe their loved one meant to commit suicide while withdrawing.

| *"[Addiction] would have cost me my life, if not for rehab."*

# Rehab Centers Can Cure Addicts

*Sarah Ewing*

*Sarah Ewing is a regular contributor to* Fabulous Magazine *in which the following viewpoint appears. Using her own experiences, she argues that drug rehabilitation centers can offer effective cures for addicts. She explains the toll alcoholism had on her life and the process of overcoming that addiction through a month-long stay at an in-house rehab center. Ewing insists that the combination of community fellowship, therapy, and medical intervention provided by the rehab center were the keys to her success.*

As you read, consider the following questions:

1. What percentage of the rehab center's clients were women during the author's stay?
2. Why does the admitting nurse require the author to remove most of her clothing immediately after admittance?

3. How old was the author when her father died?

I've always partied hard and I was famous for never leaving a bottle of booze unfinished.

But what started as social drinking while I was working in London spiralled out of control when I relocated to Pembrokeshire in 1999 to run my own company.

## Pre-Rehab

I had been hitting the bottle harder than usual since the death of my father four years previously, and the pressure of running my own business, coupled with supporting my mother through breast cancer, soon saw me going on all-day benders and even driving drunk.

By this time last year [2007] I was having regular blackouts, and terrifying family and friends by going missing for days at a time.

I'd been abusing my body for 15 years and it started to shut down.

I was teetering on the edge of bankruptcy—I'd become so drink-dependent I'd run my business into the ground and my house was about to be repossessed.

I knew I was at rock bottom and needed help.

So last July [2008] I used the remains of my savings to check into the £1,500-a-week Lynwode alcohol rehabilitation centre in Barnsley, Yorkshire.

This is what happened . . .

## Week One

I am filled with anxiety as I walk towards a small stately home.

Although it looks like a hotel, it's a clinic—and my last chance to kick the alcohol addiction that is slowly killing me.

I'm nervous about what lies ahead but determined to succeed.

I check-in with the rest of the 'guests'—my fellow alcoholics.

Half of us are women, half men, aged between 20 and 65.

I have to strip down to my bra and pants so a nurse can see I'm not concealing any alcohol, then I'm shown to my room which is sunny and welcoming.

Finally, I'm going to get the help I so badly need.

I'm put on a week's detox and have to take regular medication to help me cope with withdrawal symptoms.

I'm in lockdown, meaning I can only stroll in the grounds under supervision in case I try to drink.

Although I have the shakes, I'm not sick, and thanks to daily counselling and medication, the alcohol cravings aren't as bad as I'd expected.

On my first full day I'm able to say those crucial words:

"I'm an alcoholic and I'm ready to accept help."

## Week Two

I'd forgotten how delicious food can be.

For years I've just eaten whatever came to hand, mid-alcoholic binge.

Almost all of my calories were liquid.

At Lynwode there's a big emphasis on communal eating.

We gather three times a day around the big kitchen table and enjoy fresh, healthy food.

In the morning we have an hour-long group therapy session.

I admit to the others, and myself, my weakness for alcohol has made me dishonest and manipulative.

I once escaped a drink-drive charge after giving a sob story to police about being ill and needing to get to hospital.

I also constantly lied to friends and family about the scale of my problem.

Opening up to strangers is cathartic and it feels good to talk about it.

## Drug Treatment Programs Can Work

The economic case for drug treatment's social utility—imperfect as existing treatment programs are—is surprisingly compelling. A 1993 Office of National Drug Control Policy review of the published research on treatment outcomes concluded overwhelmingly that addicts who receive treatment—even if they don't recover—impose considerably less financial burden on society. "The cost-benefit ratios were very impressive," says Dr. James Langenbucher of Rutgers University, the review's director. "The data show that for every $1 spent on treatment, between $2 and $7 are either averted in public health and criminal justice costs or gained in productivity related to resumed employment."

The most persuasive studies of the more than 50 in the review painstakingly checked each patient's past criminal, medical, and employment records. They collected data from the years both before and after treatment, allowing two vital conclusions: that the changes observed after treatment truly were a result of the treatment, and that the benefits persisted after the patient completed or dropped out of treatment.

*Sally Satel, "Yes, Drug Treatment Can Work,"*
City Journal, *Summer 1995.*

I still have the shakes but my withdrawal has been mild compared to some others, who barely sleep and suffer excruciating headaches.

## Week Three

There is a close bond forming within our group.

It really feels like we're all in this together.

I'm now sharing a room with another woman.

This 'buddy system' is meant to encourage us to share our experiences.

And it does—we stay up until the early hours talking.

It's great to meet people who are like me and don't judge me.

We're allowed visitors, but I've told my family and friends I don't want to see them.

They understand.

After years of being strong for them, I need to focus on me and on getting well again.

But I'm not lonely.

We're already like one big family in here.

## Week Four

I've told my therapists everything.

How I was a high-powered City girl who drank for business and pleasure, and how I believed that as long as I hit my work targets, alcohol was still my friend.

My father died when I was 28 and I was too busy to grieve for him, so I parcelled up the pain and put it away.

Then my mother developed breast cancer and I was by her side as she went through months of gruelling chemotherapy before finally being given the all-clear.

I told them that I was the kind of person who gave 150 per cent to everything, including drinking.

They told me I had to stop blaming other people and other things for my alcohol addiction.

They said I was like a lot of alcoholics, controlling and oversensitive, so that when I was faced with things I couldn't handle—like my dad's death—I turned to drink.

Alcohol had been my crutch, but it had finally destroyed me.

After a month in rehab I'm ready to leave.

On my last day I feel euphoric—it's my first natural high in years.

I feel free of my old life, as if the slate has been wiped clean.

A friend comes to pick me up and drives me to Glastonbury, where I plan to make a fresh start as a yoga instructor.

## Postscript

Eight months later I am teetotal, and as happy and carefree as the day I left Lynwode.

Addiction cost me my business, my home and my financial security.

It would have cost me my life, if not for rehab.

I'm single and enjoying living without booze.

Although I still go out with friends, I have swapped vodka for mineral water and enjoyed my first sober Christmas in years.

I'm not tempted to drink.

Even the smell of alcohol reminds me of those dark days when I was addicted to it.

I also feel and look much healthier.

I'm fitter, and my skin is no longer pale and pasty.

I'm teaching yoga and also training to be a counsellor so I can help others like me.

| "Didn't she know she was killing herself?"

# Medical Rehab Centers Cannot Cure Addicts

*Anna B. Reisman*

*When Anna B. Reisman first met Sylvia Cleary, she looked like a normal secretary. She did not look at all like an alcoholic. The truth was Cleary had been abusing alcohol for more than ten years. She would battle the disease of alcoholism for several more years, eventually succumbing to cirrhosis. The following viewpoint argues that physicians cannot do much to help alcoholics, regardless of whether they are high-functioning or not. Reisman is a doctor and a contributor to* The Hastings Center Report.

As you read, consider the following questions:

1. What is cirrhosis and what is one of the most common causes of it?
2. What is Librium?
3. According to Reisman, what can physicians do to help alcoholic patients?

Anna B. Reisman, "Saving Sylvia Cleary," *The Hastings Center Report*, vol. 37, July-August 2007, pp. 9–10. Copyright © 2007 Hastings Center. Reproduced by permission.

Sylvia Cleary rolled up the sleeves of her starched white blouse to show me a few pale, blotchy bruises on her forearms. A soft-spoken forty-six-year-old secretary who wore a red A-line skirt and decorated her dark brown bob with rhinestone barrettes, she had come to my clinic at Bellevue Hospital with a sense, as she put it, that something was metabolically wrong. I reassured her that plenty of people bruise themselves without realizing it.

The results of her routine blood tests were puzzling. There was marked inflammation of the liver, possibly cirrhosis. To me, an inexperienced intern, it seemed unlikely that alcohol—one of the most common causes of cirrhosis—had anything to do with the bruises.

## The Truth

A week later, Ms. Cleary was back for her blood test results. A few questions revealed that she'd been drinking at least a pint of scotch a day for more than ten years. It was hard to believe. She seemed so reasonable, so together. Perhaps, with my guidance, she could give up drinking.

I reminded myself what I'd learned in medical school lectures: alcoholism is a disease. I chose my words carefully. I didn't want to scare her away.

"The scotch," I said, "is damaging your liver. The bruises are a sign of this. You really need to think about resisting the urge to drink."

She nodded, rubbed her hands together. "I'll have to do it, then."

Going cold turkey could be dangerous; even a small change could trigger a withdrawal seizure. I asked her to consider the hospital's inpatient detox program.

"I'd rather do it myself," she said: "I can handle it."

## Worrying About a Patient

I worried about her over the next few days and decided to give her a call. I'd find out if she was okay, and a few words of encouragement might help her stay on track. The first time I called, she reassured me that things were fine. She was cutting down without any problem. The second time, she told me not to worry and said she'd see me in a month. I picked up the phone several times during the next three weeks, but at the last minute I'd hang up before dialing.

I told my attending physician about my concern over Ms. Cleary. Let the baby bird out of the nest, he said. The phrase seemed a little abrupt. It may have made sense for some patients, like the down-and-out alcoholics—the disheveled, smelly, ornery men who'd show up in the ER trembling and feverish after spending the last of their disability checks on booze days earlier. With them, I'd go through the motions mechanically: the statement of the obvious ("You're an alcoholic, and you're destroying your liver."); the taper of Librium, a medication that mimicked the effects of alcohol in a safe, controllable way; the Alcoholics Anonymous [AA] recommendation; the clinic appointment for follow-up that was never kept. Other than easing their withdrawal symptoms, I couldn't help them. But for high-functioning addicts like Ms. Cleary, didn't I need to do more?

## Attempts to Get Sober

A month later, we were both beaming. Ms. Cleary had completely stopped drinking scotch.

Her secret, she confided, the flush in her cheeks matching the color of her cranberry jumper, was wine—she believed that it was less damaging to her liver.

My smile froze. I pulled my chair closer to hers. To the liver, I explained, struggling to keep my tone even, alcohol is alcohol. Her healthy pink glow, I noticed, was actually a filigree of burst capillaries, another sign of liver disease. I asked her again to consider inpatient detox. She was as reluctant as before, but when I pointed out that the timing was good—

she'd just left one job and had a few weeks before she planned to start temping—she agreed to give it a try.

I went up to the detox unit a few days later. She was a bit groggy from the Librium but appeared upbeat about the experience. The only woman there, she was enjoying the attention. "The guys are so polite," she whispered, smiling at a heavyset, grizzled man shuffling by. "They insist on carrying my meal tray."

She leaned down to pull up a ruffled sock, her face partially hidden, and told me that she was checking out early. She had lined up a job interview and couldn't miss it. I asked her to consider staying. She said she'd be fine.

She called a few weeks later to report that she was still sober. It wasn't easy, she said. For awhile, she couldn't find an AA group that she liked. One day, in a foul mood, she picked up a pile of Chinese restaurant menus that littered the floor of her lobby, marched down the street to the restaurant, and threw them inside. That same evening she found herself walking toward the liquor store but on the way decided to give AA one more try. I hadn't been aware of the variation: there were groups that catered to the elderly, teenagers, singles, agnostics. She giggled: the one she found that night was a gay men's group. She loved it.

Three months passed before Ms. Cleary's January appointment. When I saw her in the waiting room, I was horrified. She looked as if she were in the late stages of pregnancy. Her ankles and feet bulged with so much fluid that, despite the frigid weather, she was wearing bedroom slippers. Her frilly blouse clung to the sides of her distended belly. In between moments of nodding off, Ms. Cleary told me how she'd gone to a few more AA meetings, but when she'd lost the job a month earlier, she'd started drinking again. It's ruining me, she said, motioning to her belly and legs. She had already cut

Project MATCH Treatment Approaches

*All patients were randomly assigned to one of three treatment approaches:*

| Type of Treatment | Goal of Treatment | Description | Frequency |
|---|---|---|---|
| CBT (Cognitive Behavioral Therapy) | Learn skills to achieve and maintain sobriety | Coping and drink-refusal skills taught by therapist to handle states and situations known to precipitate relapse | 12 weekly sessions |
| TSF (Twelve Step Facilitation) | Acceptance of the disease of alcoholism and loss of control over drinking | Patients introduced by therapist to the first steps of Alcoholics Anonymous and encouraged to attend meetings | 12 weekly sessions |
| MET (Motivational Enhancement Therapy) | Mobilize the person's own commitment and motivation to change | Therapist applies motivational psychology to examine effect of drinking on patient's life, and develop and implement a plan to stop drinking | 4 sessions in 12 weeks |

TAKEN FROM: Butler Center for Research, "Project MATCH: A study of Alcoholism Treatment Approaches," *Research Update*, Hazelden Foundation, June 2000.

back to a couple glasses every few days and was planning on quitting for good. Could I give her something for the swelling?

I wanted to shake her. Didn't she know she was killing herself? Trying to maintain my composure, I told her that she needed to get it together and quit or she would die. She swore that this time she would really stop, for good, no matter what it took. I wanted to believe her. I arranged an appointment with the liver clinic and prescribed some diuretics. She took my hand to thank me, clinging to it for a second too long.

Two weeks later, she had lost five pounds. I could almost make out the shape of her ankles.

After that, Ms. Cleary stopped coming to clinic. I called her several times to remind her of her appointments. She never called back. Maybe she had started drinking again. Maybe she had succumbed to her cirrhosis. Or perhaps she'd simply moved away, found a job that offered medical insurance, switched to a private physician. One night, I dreamed that a college friend had become a heroin addict. I called him to tell him he should quit. F--- you, he said. Was that what Ms. Cleary was trying to tell me? After she'd missed three more appointments, I decided that for one reason or another, she didn't want to see me anymore.

## Advanced Cirrhosis

More than a year later, in the beginning of my third year of residency, Ms. Cleary paged me. This was resourceful; it wasn't easy for a patient to get access to the paging system. She had wanted to call months earlier but worried that she had let me down. But in the last week she'd felt bloated and exhausted. I was glad to have another chance to help. Since I wouldn't be back in clinic for a few weeks, I recommended that she see one of my fellow residents the next afternoon.

Three days after, I heard that Ms. Cleary was in the intensive care unit. My heart sank when I saw her. Her skin was deep saffron, the unmistakable color of end-stage liver disease. She was holding up a hand mirror and reapplying her lipstick. When she noticed me, she flashed a wide smile. She filled me in on the past year's events: steady work had made it impossible for her to get to the Bellevue clinic; a pharmacist friend had been refilling her diuretics. A couple of months earlier, after a relationship failed, she had started drinking again. After we spoke on the phone a few days earlier, she had decided to wait until she could see me. Two days later she'd vomited blood, passed out, and ended up in the ICU. I felt a lump in my throat. How could I have ignored what was staring at me in the face? The bruises, the broken blood vessels: even back when I first met her, she was an end-stage alcoholic with advanced cirrhosis.

With a giddy laugh, Ms. Cleary admitted that she really had gotten the message this time. She felt truly ready to stop drinking forever.

I blinked back tears when I saw her the next day. Her dark yellow wrists flapped as she reached for my hand. She had disappeared for so long and now she was dying in front of me. She still recognized me but chatted with unseen creatures as well.

There was nothing left to do. She lay on her back, eyes closed, mouth open, her musty odor filling the room. A basin of her bloody vomit was balanced on the sink.

The next morning her bed was empty.

What is the physician's role with a high-functioning alcoholic? The truth is that whether the patient is a skid row bum or a neatly dressed secretary, we can't do much. But here's what we can do: we can start an unbiased conversation about alcohol—forge a connection. We can ask about the disease when no one else will. Our potential with alcoholic patients may be limited, but there is also opportunity.

> *"Addicts seem to benefit from being in a room with people who understand what they have been through."*

# Group Approaches Are Effective at Breaking Addiction to Alcohol

### Dirk Hanson

*Dirk Hanson is the author of several books, including* Addiction: The Search for a Cure. *In the following viewpoint he argues that Alcoholics Anonymous (AA) is successful in helping alcoholics overcome addiction because the group dynamic promotes a sense of community. He asserts that alcoholics cannot combat the disease alone and that the founders of AA were aware of the need for support in the process of recovery. Furthermore, Hanson acknowledges that seeking help from others is not an attempt to avoid responsibility for addictive behavior but a way to tap into a force larger than oneself.*

As you read, consider the following questions:

1. Who is Bill Wilson?
2. What is the "Big Book"?
3. What is "hitting bottom"?

Dirk Hanson, "Does AA Work?" www.dirkhanson.org, 2007. Reproduced by permission.

Despite recent progress in the medical understanding of addictive disease, the amateur self-help group known as Alcoholics Anonymous [A.A.], and its affiliate, Narcotics Anonymous, are still regarded by many as the most effective mode of treatment for the ex-addict who is serious about keeping his or her disease in remission. . . .

Under the biochemical paradigm of addiction, we have to ask whether the common A.A.-style of group rehabilitation . . . [is] nothing more than brainwashing combined with a covert pitch for some of that old-time religion. As Dr. Arnold Ludwig has phrased it, "Why should alcoholism, unlike any other 'disease,' be regarded as relatively immune to medical or psychiatric intervention and require, as A.A. principles insist, a personal relationship with a Higher Power as an essential element for recovery?" The notion is reminiscent of earlier moralistic approaches to the problem, often couched in strictly religious terms. It conjures up the approach sometimes taken by fundamentalist Christians, in which a conversion experience in the name of Jesus is considered the only possible route to rehabilitation.

But if all this is so, why do so many of the hardest of hard scientists in the field continue to recommend A.A. meetings as part of treatment? Desperation? Even researchers and therapists who don't particularly like anything about the A.A. program often reluctantly recommend it, in the absence of any cheap alternatives.

## History of A.A.

In 1939, Bill Wilson and the fellowship of non-drinkers that had coalesced around him published the basic textbook of the movement, *Alcoholics Anonymous*. The book retailed for $3.50, a bit steep for the times, so Bill W. compensated by having it printed on the thickest paper available—hence its nickname, the "Big Book." The foreword to the first printing stated: "We are not an organization in the conventional sense of the word.

There are no fees or dues whatsoever. The only requirement for membership is an honest desire to stop drinking. We are not allied with any particular faith, sect or denomination, nor do we oppose anyone. We simply wish to be helpful to those who are afflicted."

In short, it sounded like a recipe for complete disaster: naïve, hopeful, objective, beyond politics, burdened with an anarchical structure, no official recordkeeping, and a membership composed of anonymous, first-name-only alcoholics.

Amid dozens of case histories of alcoholics, the Big Book contained the original Twelve Steps toward physical and spiritual recovery. There are also Twelve Traditions, the fourth one being, "Each group should be autonomous except in matters affecting other groups or A.A. as a whole." As elaborated upon in Twelve Steps and Twelve Traditions, "There would be real danger should we commence to call some groups 'wet' or 'dry,' still others 'Republican' or 'Communist'. . . . Sobriety had to be its sole objective. In all other respects there was perfect freedom of will and action. Every group had the right to be wrong. The unofficial Rule #62 was: 'Don't take yourself too damn seriously!'"

As a well-known celebrity in A.A. put it: "In Bill W.'s last talk, he was asked what the most important aspect of the program was, and he said it was the principle of anonymity. It's the spiritual foundation." Co-founder Dr. Bob, for his part, believed the essence of the Twelve Steps could be distilled into two words—"love" and "service." This clearly links the central thrust of A.A. to religious and mystical practices, although it is easily viewed in strictly secular terms, too. Alcoholics Anonymous recounts a conversation "our friend" had with [psychoanalyst] Dr. C.G. Jung. Once in a while, Jung wrote, ". . . alcoholics have had what are called vital spiritual experiences. . . . They appear to be in the nature of huge emotional displacements and rearrangements." As stated in Twelve Steps and Twelve Traditions, "Nearly every serious emotional problem can be seen as a case of misdirected instinct. When that happens, our great natural assets, the instincts, have turned into physical and mental liabilities."

Alcoholics Anonymous asserts that there are times when the addict "has no effective mental defense" against that first drink.

Bill Wilson wrote:

> Some strongly object to the A.A. position that alcoholism is an illness. This concept, they feel, removes moral responsibility from alcoholics. As any A.A. knows, this is far from true. We do not use the concept of sickness to absolve our members from responsibility. On the contrary, we use the fact of fatal illness to clamp the heaviest kind of moral obligation onto the sufferer, the obligation to use A.A.'s Twelve Steps to get well.

(For A.A. detractors, see Stanton Peele's *The Diseasing of America*, Herbert Fingarette's *Heavy Drinking*, or *Seven Weeks to Safe Social Drinking* by Donna Cornett.)

## Hitting Bottom

This excruciating state of moral and physical sickness—this "incomprehensible demoralization"—is known in A.A. as hitting bottom. "Why is it," asks Dr. Arnold Ludwig, "that reasonably intelligent men and women remain relatively immune to reason and good advice and only choose to quit drinking when they absolutely must, after so much damage has been wrought? What is there about alcoholism, unlike any other 'disease' in medicine except certain drug addictions, that makes being in extremis represent a potentially favorable sign for cure?"

Hitting bottom may come in the form of a wrecked car, a wrecked marriage, a jail term, or simply the inexorable buildup of the solo burden of drug-seeking behavior. While the intrinsically spiritual component of the A.A. program would seem

# The Twelve Steps

The heart of the suggested program of personal recovery is contained in Twelve Steps:

1. We admitted we were powerless over alcohol—that our lives had become unmanageable.

2. Came to believe that a Power greater than ourselves could restore us to sanity.

3. Made a decision to turn our will and our lives over to the care of God *as we understood Him.*

4. Made a searching and fearless moral inventory of ourselves.

5. Admitted to God, to ourselves and to another human being the exact nature of our wrongs.

6. Were entirely ready to have God remove all these defects of character.

7. Humbly asked Him to remove our shortcomings.

8. Made a list of all persons we had harmed, and became willing to make amends to them all.

9. Made direct amends to such people wherever possible, except when to do so would injure them or others.

10. Continued to take personal inventory and when we were wrong promptly admitted it.

11. Sought through prayer and meditation to improve our conscious contact with God *as we understood Him,* praying only for knowledge of His will for us and the power to carry that out.

12. Having had a spiritual awakening as the result of these steps, we tried to carry this message to alcoholics and to practice these principles in all our affairs.

"A.A. Factfile,"
*General Service Office of Alcoholics Anonymous, April 2005.*

to be inconsistent with the emerging biochemical models of addiction, recall that A.A.'s basic premise has always been that alcoholism and drug addiction are diseases of the body and obsessions of the mind.

When the shocking moment arrives, and the addict hits bottom, he or she enters a "sweetly reasonable" and "softened up" state of mind, as A.A. founder Bill Wilson expressed it. Arnold Ludwig calls this the state of "therapeutic surrender." It is crucial to everything that follows. It is the stage in their lives when addicts are prepared to consider, if only as a highly disturbing hypothesis, that they have become powerless over their use of addictive drugs. In that sense, their lives have become unmanageable. They have lost control.

A.A.'s contention that there is a power greater than the self can be seen in cybernetic terms—that is to stay, in strictly secular terms. As systems theorist Gregory Bateson concluded after an examination of A.A principles in *Steps to an Ecology of Mind*:

> The 'self' as ordinarily understood is only a small part of a much larger trial-and-error system which does the thinking, acting and deciding ... The 'self' is a false reification of an improperly delimited part of this much larger field of interlocking processes. Cybernetics also recognizes that two or more persons—any group of persons—may together form such a thinking-and-acting system.

Therefore, it isn't necessary to take a strictly spiritual view in order to recognize the existence of some kind of power higher than the self. The higher power referred to in A.A. may simply turn out to be the complex dynamics of directed group interaction, i.e., the group as a whole. It is a recognition of holistic processes beyond a single individual—the power of the many over and against the power of one. Sometimes that form of submission can be healthy. Addicts seem to benefit from being in a room with people who understand what they have been through, and the changes they are now facing. It is useful to know that they are not alone in this. "The unit of survival—either in ethics or in evolution—is not the organism or the species," wrote Bateson, "but the largest system or 'power' within which the creature lives." In behavioral terms, A.A. enshrines this sophisticated understanding as a first principle.

# Periodical Bibliography

*The following articles have been selected to supplement the diverse views presented in this chapter.*

Hal Arkowitz and Scott Lilienfield — "D.I.Y. Addiction Cures?" *Scientific Mind*, vol. 19, no. 4, 2008.

*CNS Disorders Today* — "Buprenorphine Helps Patients Kick Opioid Addiction," September 20, 2008.

Matthew Herper — "Tobacco-Free," *Forbes*, December 10, 2007.

*Inpharma Weekly* — "Drug Addiction: A New Hope?" May 3, 2008.

Jeneen Interlandi and Raina Kelley — "What Addicts Need," *Newsweek*, March 3, 2008.

Danny Kushlick — "Stopping the Conveyor Belt to Addiction," *New Statesman*, May 18, 2007.

John G. Lovelace — "Making the Recovery Model Real," *Behavioral Healthcare*, December 2007.

Lisa Merlo and Mark S. Gold — "Addiction Research and Treatment," *Psychiatric Times*, June 2008.

*Science News* — "It's Time for Addiction Science to Supersede Stigma," November 8, 2008.

*Woman's Day* — "Time to Unplug," September 8, 2008.

# For Further Discussion

## Chapter 1

1. Howard J. Schaffer offers an operational definition for addiction. Do you agree or disagree with his criteria?

2. Dale Netherton argues that addicts choose to abuse alcohol and drugs, while Kevin T. McCauley argues that addiction is a disease over which alcoholics have little control. After reading each viewpoint, do you think alcoholism is a disease or a choice? How does each viewpoint influence your understanding of the issue?

3. John G. Messerly and Nick Yee's viewpoints are in response to recent controversies about the negative effects of online gaming. Based on the evidence each author provides, do you think players can become addicted to online games? Why or why not?

4. What evidence does Stanton Peele give in defense of the addictive properties of marijuana? What evidence does Robert Volkman give in support of the lack of addictive properties of marijuana? Whose viewpoint do you find more convincing, and why?

## Chapter 2

1. Nan Einarson argues that by introducing alcohol in the home, fewer young people will abuse alcohol. Teen Drug Rehab Treatment Centers asserts that there is little evidence that introducing young people to alcohol in the home has any positive effects on alcohol use. After reading these two viewpoints, do you think parents should introduce their children to alcohol in the home setting?

2. Joseph R. McKinney and Ryan Grim debate the success of random student drug testing in schools. Which viewpoint offers the strongest evidence? Explain your answer.

## Chapter 3

1. Rae Hoffman argues that using electronic communication tools can help friends and family stay in touch. Diane K. Danielson argues that too much dependence on these devices can lead to lack of actual communication between couples. Based on the evidence presented, how do you think dependence on online communication affects relationships?

2. Daniel Weiss argues that pornography addiction can lead to violence against women. Based on the evidence he provides, can you imagine circumstances in which this might be the case? Or do you agree with Daniel Linz who asserts that not only does the consumption of pornography not lead to violence against women, but it is not addictive in the first place?

3. A dentist with the Michigan Dental Association argues that Alcoholics Anonymous (AA) can save a marriage, while Mary Barrett argues that AA can present a challenge to couples struggling with alcohol abuse. Based on these viewpoints, do you think AA can help couples maintain their marriages? Explain your answer.

## Chapter 4

1. What evidence does Barry Nelson use to argue that drug clinics can be effective in treating heroin addiction? What evidence does Jean Sparks-Carreker offer to argue that drug clinics cannot cure all opiate addictions? Whose viewpoint is more convincing to you, and why?

2. Sarah Ewing asserts that rehabilitation centers offer the most effective treatment for addiction, while Anna B. Reisman argues that medical rehab centers do not help most addicts. Which viewpoint is more persuasive? Explain your answer.

3. Dirk Hanson argues the usefulness of groups in fighting substance abuse. Based on the evidence offered, do you think group therapy can be beneficial for addicts?

# Organizations to Contact

*The editors have compiled the following list of organizations concerned with the issues debated in this book. The descriptions are derived from materials provided by the organizations. All have publications or information available for interested readers. The list was compiled on the date of publication of the present volume; the information provided here may change. Be aware that many organizations take several weeks or longer to respond to inquiries, so allow as much time as possible.*

**Adult Children of Alcoholics (ACA)**
PO Box 3216, Torrance, CA   90510
(310) 534-1815
e-mail: info@adultchildren.org
Web site: http://adultchildren.org

Adult Children of Alcoholics (ACA) is a nonprofit organization devoted to supporting adult children of alcoholics and otherwise dysfunctional families. Using the twelve-step program developed by Alcoholics Anonymous, ACA helps its members better understand how their childhood experiences affect their adult relationships. In addition to education pamphlets, ACA also publishes workbooks and *ComLine*, a monthly newsletter.

**Al-Anon/Alateen**
1600 Corporate Landing Parkway
Virginia Beach, VA   23454-5617
(757) 563-1600 • fax: (757) 563-1655
e-mail: wso@al-anon.org
Web site: www.al-anon.alateen.org

Al-Anon is an international organization devoted to helping families and friends of alcoholics cope. Their sub-group, Alateen, is specifically geared towards the needs of teenagers who have been affected by alcoholism. While Al-Anon/Alateen's primary function is to provide opportunities for the formation of support groups, they also publish educational literature, such as their most recent book, *Discovering Choices*, and a newsletter, *The Forum*.

## Alcoholics Anonymous (AA)
PO Box 459, New York, NY   10163
(212) 870-3400
Web site: www.aa.org

Alcoholics Anonymous (AA) is an international organization that provides support for people trying to quit abusing alcohol. AA was founded in 1935 and focuses on a twelve-step program to help its members fight addiction. AA's most well-known publication is called *The Big Book*. It also publishes pamphlets and other materials to educate and support its members.

## American Society of Addiction Medicine (ASAM)
4601 N. Park Avenue, Upper Arcade #101
Chevy Chase, MD   20815
(301) 656-3920 • fax: (301) 656 3815
e-mail: email@asam.org
Web site: www.asam.org

American Society of Addiction Medicine (ASAM) is an organization of researchers, physicians, and other professionals who seek to educate health care providers and the public about ways of treating and preventing addiction. It carries out its mission by sponsoring research and publishing annual reports. ASAM also regularly publishes *The Journal of Addiction Medicine* and *ASAM News*.

## Narconon International
262 Gaffey Road, Watsonville, CA   95076
(800) 556-8885 • fax: (831) 768-7194
e-mail: info@drugrehab.net
Web site: www.narconon.org

Founded in 1966, Narconon International is a nonprofit organization devoted to helping clients overcome their addiction to drugs. It is a network of over 120 drug prevention and drug-free social education rehabilitation centers. Narconon regularly sponsors drug research and produces books and videos to educate the public about drug use. Some of their most recent titles include *The Truth About Drugs: What Is It?* and *Marijuana: The Myth.*

**National Association for Children of Alcoholics (NACoA)**
11426 Rockville Pike, Suite 301, Rockville, Maryland 20852
(888) 55-4COAS • fax: (301) 468-0985
e-mail: nacoa@nacoa.org
Web site: www.naco.org

The National Association for Children of Alcoholics (NACoA) is a nonprofit organization that advocates for children of parents who are dependent on alcohol and drugs. It accomplishes its mission by raising public awareness of the affects of parental drug dependence on children and by influencing legislation on local and federal levels. NACoA regularly publishes informative articles and booklets such as *A Family Guide: Alcohol, Tobacco, Other Drugs and Teenagers* and *Children of Alcoholics: Selected Readings.*

**National Council on Alcoholism and Drug Dependence (NCADD)**
244 East Fifty-Eighth Street 4th Floor, New York, NY 10022
(212) 269-212/269-7510
e-mail: national@ncadd.org
Web site: http://www.ncadd.org

Founded in 1944, National Council on Alcoholism and Drug Dependence (NCADD) provides education, information, and assistance to the public and health care providers about alcohol and drug addiction. It advocates prevention, intervention, and treatment through a nationwide network of affiliates. In addition to videos, posters, and fact sheets, NCADD publishes brochures such as "What Are the Signs of Alcoholism?" and "What Can You Do About Someone Else's Drinking?"

## National Institute on Drug Abuse (NIDA)

6001 Executive Boulevard, Room 5213
Bethesda, MD   20892-9561
(301) 443-1124
e-mail: information@nida.nih.gov
Web site: www.nida.nih.gov

The mission of the National Institute on Drug Abuse (NIDA) as a sub-group of the National Institutes of Health is to use science to help understand and treat drug addiction. It accomplishes this goal by sponsoring and disseminating research and by working with legislators and other lawmakers through their advisory group, the National Advisory Council on Drug Abuse. In addition to fact sheets and brief research reports, NIDA publishes books, including *Marijuana: Facts for Teens* and *Drugs, Brains, and Behavior: The Science of Addiction.*

## Nicotine Anonymous (NicA)

419 Main Street, PMB# 370, Huntington Beach, CA   92648
(877) 879-6422
e-mail: info@nicotine-anonymous.org
Web site: www.nicotine-anonymous.org

Nicotine Anonymous (NicA) is a national support organization that uses the twelve-step program developed by Alcoholics Anonymous to help members quit smoking. In addition to many regular meetings across the country, NicA offers outreach services to community members addicted to nicotine. Its most recent publications include pamphlets such as *The Serenity Prayer for Nicotine Users* and *Tips for Gaining Freedom from Nicotine.*

## Overeaters Anonymous (OA)

PO Box 44020, Rio Rancho, NM   87174-4020
(505) 891-2664 • (505) 891-4320
e-mail: info@oa.org
Web site: www.oa.org

Founded in 1960, Overeaters Anonymous (OA) is a national support group that uses the twelve-step program developed by Alcoholics Anonymous to help members better understand their struggles with a variety of disordered eating behaviors. In addition to regular group meetings across the country, OA provides outreach services and education to the public. In addition to *Courier*, a monthly newsletter for professionals, OA publishes *Lifeline Magazine*.

**Secular Organizations for Sobriety (SOS)**
4773 Hollywood Blvd, Hollywood, CA   90027
(323) 666-4295 • fax: (323) 666-4271
e-Mail: SOS@CFIWest.org

Secular Organizations for Sobriety (SOS) is a nonprofit network of autonomous, nonprofessional local groups in the United States and many European countries dedicated to helping individuals achieve and maintain sobriety. SOS began as a secular alternative to sobriety programs focused on God or some other higher power. The SOS Web site includes a number of resources, including online support groups, a sobriety tool kit, and articles, such as "Factors in the Causation and Development of Alcoholism" and "Drugs and Cross Addiction."

**Sexual Compulsives Anonymous (SCA)**
PO Box 1585, Old Chelsea Station, New York, NY   10011
800-977-HEAL
Web site: www.sca-recovery.org

Sexual Compulsives Anonymous (SCA) is a national support organization that uses the twelve-step program developed by Alcoholics Anonymous to help members overcome sexual compulsion. In addition to many regular meetings across the country, SCA offers outreach services to community members and educates the public about sex addiction. Its most recent publications include *Sexual Compulsives Anonymous: A Program of Recovery "The Little Blue Book"* and *The SCAnner* newsletter.

# Bibliography of Books

Peter J. Adams    *Fragmented Intimacy: Addiction in a Social World.* New York: Springer, 2008.

Bruce Alexander    *The Globalisation of Addiction.* New York: Oxford University Press, 2008.

Marina Barnard    *Drug Addiction and Families.* London: Jessica Kingsley, 2007.

Trevor Bennett and Katy Holloway    *Understanding Drugs, Alcohol and Crime.* New York: Open University Press, 2005.

Carol Bucciarelli    *Addicted and Mentally Ill: Stories of Courage, Hope, and Empowerment.* New York: Haworth Press, 2005.

Allen Carr    *The Easy Way to Stop Drinking.* New York: Sterling, 2005.

Susan Cheever    *Desire: Where Sex Meets Addiction.* New York: Simon & Schuster, 2008.

Carlo C. DiClemente    *Addiction and Change: How Addictions Develop and Addicted People Recover.* New York: Guilford Press, 2003.

John C. Fleming    *Preventing Addiction.* New York: Crosshouse, 2006.

Sharon A. Hersh    *The Last Addiction: Why Self Help Is Not Enough, Own Your Desire, Live Beyond Recovery, Find Lasting Freedom.* Colorado Springs, CO: WaterBrook Press, 2008.

John Hoffman and Susan Froemke, eds.

*Addiction: Why Can't They Just Stop?: New Knowledge, New Treatments, New Hope.* New York: Rodale, 2007.

Morteza Khaleghi

*Free from Addiction: Facing Yourself and Embracing Recovery.* New York: Palgrave Macmillan, 2008.

Stephen A. Maisto, Gerard J. Connors, Ronda L. Dearing

*Alcohol Use Disorders.* Toronto: Hogrefe and Huber, 2007.

Gerald G. May

*Addiction and Grace: Love and Spirituality in the Healing of Addictions.* San Francisco, CA: HarperSanFrancisco, 2006.

William G. McCown and William A. Howatt

*Treating Gambling Problems.* Hoboken, NJ: John Wiley and Sons, 2007.

Sheryl Letzgus McGinnis

*Slaying the Addiction Monster: An All-Inclusive Look at Drug Addiction in America Today.* New York: BookSurge, 2008.

William R. Miller and Kathleen M. Carroll, eds.

*Rethinking Substance Abuse: What the Science Shows, and What We Should Do About It.* New York: Guilford Press, 2006.

M.A. Moe

*Understanding Addiction and Recovery Through a Child's Eyes: Hope, Help, and Healing for Families.* New York: HCI, 2007.

Susan Peabody — *Addiction to Love: Overcoming Obsession and Dependency in Relationships.* New York: Celestial Arts, 2005.

Stanton Peele — *Seven Tools to Beat Addiction.* New York: Three Rivers Press, 2004.

Moira Plant and Martin Plant, eds. — *Addiction.* New York: Routledge, 2008.

Chris Prentiss — *The Alcoholism and Addiction Cure: A Holistic Approach to Total Recovery.* Los Angeles: Power Press, 2005.

John Howard Prin — *Secret Keeping: Overcoming Hidden Habits and Addictions.* New York: New World Library, 2006.

Rao S. Rapaka and Wolfgang Sadée, eds. — *Drug Addiction: From Basic Research to Therapy.* New York: Springer, 2008.

David Sheff — *Beautiful Boy: A Father's Journey Through His Son's Addiction.* Boston, MA: Houghton Mifflin, 2008.

Kevin B. Skinner — *Treating Pornography Addiction: The Essential Tools for Recovery.* New York: GrowthClimate, 2005.

Jill Talbot — *Loaded: Women and Addiction.* Emeryville, CA: Seal, 2007.

Vatsal G. Thakkar — *Addiction.* New York: Chelsea House, 2006.

Darin Weinberg    *Of Others Inside: Insanity, Addiction, and Belonging in America.* Philadelphia, PA: Temple University Press, 2005.

# Index